The Total Film-Maker

The
Total
Film-Maker

by

JERRY LEWIS

VISION

Vision Press Limited

157 Knightsbridge

London SW1X 7PA

ISBN 0 85478 023 8

First published in the British Commonwealth 1974
© 1971 by Jerry Lewis

Printed in Great Britain by
Clarke, Doble & Brendon Ltd., Plymouth
MCMLXXIV

To my lady: Patti
Whose love, patience and wisdom
never diminished
while waiting for me to grow up

ACKNOWLEDGMENTS

My sincere thanks to Dr. Bernie Kantor, Professor Arthur Knight, Professor Irwin Blacket and Anne Kramer for their inspiration.

And to my students who taught me so much about teaching, especially Peter Arnold, Dicil Walters and Alan Swyer.

Plus a deep bow to Rusty Wiles, my cutter, who, along with *every member* of my crews over the years, gave me the information and guidance that allowed me to accept the position at the U.S.C. Cinema Department with a feeling of qualified humility.

TO THE READER

As a kid I wanted to be a writer, but at fifteen was shocked to learn there were people like Saroyan and Hemingway doing the same thing—and no matter what happened to me and my work, they persisted and went ahead without me.

Twenty-five years later I found myself teaching at the University of Southern California—no, not writing, but just about everything else having to do with making film. You can imagine my surprise when Random House wanted a book from me on the total film-maker. I said I'd write it—they said, "Don't." Upon asking, "How do I write a book without writing?" they answered, "You tape every class and your book will be everything you said, with *your* by-line."

Hence the following pages represent a half million feet of audio tape compiled, examined, listened to, transcribed and finally edited into respective categories.

I think I love films and those who love them better than just about anything else in the world—and I hope when you read this book you will become a part of the already overwhelming number of film-loving people.

J. L.

CONTENTS

The Total Film-Maker

PROLOGUE

The total film-maker is a man who gives of himself through emulsion, which in turn acts as a mirror. What he gives he gets back.

Because I believe in what can be done with film in our big round put-on, I wanted to write about it so that others, the new ones who are driven to work with it, who want to say their thing, can maybe learn something of what I've learned. So, leaving the over-thirties to wallow in their own messes, I am aiming this toward the young, the fired-up long- and short-hairs who want to lick emulsion.

Film, baby, powerful tool for love or laughter, fantastic weapon to create violence or ward it off, is in your hands.

The only possible chance you've got in our round thing is not to bitch about injustice or break windows, but to make a concerted effort to have a loud voice. The loudest voice known to man is on thousand-foot reels. Campus chants about war are not going to help two peasants in a rice paddy on Tuesday. However, something might be said on emulsion that will stop a soldier from firing into nine children somewhere, sometime. Now; next year; five years from now. Try emulsion instead of rocks for race relations and ecology. That, and love and laughter, has to be what it's all about. Then you'll survive. Maybe we'll all survive. Maybe.

Emulsion has the strangest capacity to react. It's almost like infectious hepatitis, only germ known to medical science that can't be sterilized off a needle. It picks up information germs. More than that, I really believe emulsion picks up the attitude of a film-maker's work. It actually "feels" the intangibles.

When you make a film under stress of one kind or another, emotional or mechanical, or without all the necessary information, it might still turn out to be a good film. But no one can put a finger on why it isn't an excellent film. The intangibles! If it flops completely, you can blame pressures, as if anyone wants to listen.

But the more information you have to apply to the film, the easier it is to work, create and design. That applies to making crullers, too. But there's a difference. The emulsion smells and feels happy. It will make things that are somewhat minor turn magnificent. It's part of the mystery of film-making, and no one yet has explained it. It's wrapped in adventure, excitement and, sometimes, true satisfaction.

I have a confession. Crazy. I have perched in a cutting room and licked emulsion. Maybe I thought more of me would get on to that film. I don't know. I do know that plumbers don't lick their pipes. With emulsion, it's easy to get turned on.

The film-maker's commitment to society comes only from his hope that society will see the picture. If he doesn't care what society thinks, then he's off on an ego trip, and isn't my definition of a film-maker. It doesn't matter what the subject is. It does matter *how* it is made. If the right optics aren't used, and if the actors don't function properly, and if the film-maker doesn't have a complete understanding of his function, it will bomb—whatever the subject.

You have to know all the technical crap as well as how to smell out the intangibles, then go make the birth of a simian under a Jewish gypsy lying in a truck in Fresno during a snowstorm prior to the wheat fields burning while a priest begs a rabbi to hug his foot.

Where do you start? There's no Monopoly board. *No Start. Do Not Pass Go.* I think you start out by just being there, and being curious and having the drive to make films.

More important: *make film, shoot film, run film.*

Do something.

Make film. Shoot anything.

It does not have to be sound.

It does not have to be titled.

It does not have to be color.

There is no *have to*. Just *do*.

And show it to somebody. If it is an audience of one, *do and show*, and then try it again.

That is how.

It sounds simple.

It's not. Then again, it is.

In what is to follow, I do not want to sound like I am anything other than what I am. I have no "isms." This is my own statement on film-making, my own point of view.

one

PROduction

1

THE HUMANITIES OF FILM

I'll tell you what I did to become a film-maker. I had this drive and I was curious. Of course, I was already a Jewish movie star and that helped get me on the lot. But in front of the camera, acting like a movie star. Not behind it! Then one day at Paramount, long ago, I was missing. They found me crawling around up on a catwalk over the sound stage. I had to know if the catwalks, where the electricians and grips do things and sleep, were made of two-by-fours. Were they built on a temporary basis? How did they hang them?

Next day, when I had a nine-o'clock shooting call, I was in the miniature department at eight, watching thirteen-inch submarines being photographed for a Cary Grant picture, *Destination Tokyo*. I had to understand why that submarine looked full size on the screen. They told me to go over and see Chuck Sutter in the camera department. I was friendly with all the technical guys.

Chuck showed me a twelve-inch lens and then showed me how they utilize it in the tank. Well, I didn't understand how they got the right dimensions on the sky and sea backings around the tank. It made it all look so real.

Chuck sent me over to the transparency department to look at the backings. "Well, where do these backings come from?"

"They shoot 'em," some guy says.

Then I went upstairs to see the artwork. It was almost nine-thirty when the assistant director found me. He requested, politely, for my ass to get back in front of the camera. Before the day was over, I was looking at generators out behind the recording building. Yes, generators! I'd heard about them.

"How do they work? Where do you plug that in? What does that do? Who turns it?"

Then I found out there is such a thing as an electrician. I shook his hand and bought him cigarettes. "Tell me things!" When I found out that all he did was throw a switch, I took back the cigarettes.

Day after that, I saw the assistant director on the phone. "Tomorrow's call is . . . ." And I saw the penciled sheets. "Well, who's he calling?"

"Oh, he's calling down there, the production department."

I spent weeks in the production department. They could never find me. Or I was by the camera. "Why does that turn? How does it turn to what? Where does he get the pictures they make? Why does it see people in that part, but when it turns over, I see no people? I see a black thing. What's moving? That part in front is what? It's a glass piece? A prism. Oh, I see. And why does that boom go off and I can't step off it unless they give me permission because it will swing up. Well, why does it do that?"

"Well, it's counterbalanced."

"With what?"

"Mercury."

"Oh, mercury. I see. Well, why does *he* push it? And why doesn't the other guy?"

"He can't. He's not in that union."

Laugh! Hollow!

Lights? "You have got to have all those lights?"

"Yes."

"Why?"

"Because you have to have four hundred footcandle."

"Footcandle? You have candles you bring in with your feet?"

"No, that's a light measurement."

He's serious and so am I.

So in about three years of that kind of running around *I learned a little*. It is not unlike medicine. The mystery of medicine, trying to cure and fix and find out the why, must be to doctors what film is to film-makers. They cannot start working their mystery until they have much more technical information than they ever really need. But it's there to be called on.

Then the intangibles! What are they? How many? Can I teach the intangibles of film-making? Not really. Maybe the only answer is: How do you touch another man's soul? It might develop from that. Sit down and say, You're dealing with lovely human beings. Each one of them is an individual. Each one of them in his own right a lovely, important-to-someone human being. Some will behave like turds, but you must try to understand why.

As a film-maker, you will find them influencing your actions. Perhaps the key to the intangibles is intuition. Old instinct. But the touch question when dealing with people is: How do I know when *I'm* human enough?

I'm going to use a word wrong because that's the way I want to use it, letting the language purists make funny noises and feel superior. The word I'm talking about is *humanities*. There is a great deal of confusion between *humanism*, which means a cultural attitude, and *humanity*, which really means a kindly disposition toward your fellow man. Well, for me the word *humanities* refers to the last definition—that important thing, that feeling of warmth and love and kindly disposition toward your fellow man, the way you look at him, feel about him, treat him, respect him and relate to him.

No matter how you slice it, the most critical aspect of making films is dealing with people. Whether you think he's a hero or an occasional creep, you must have a rooting interest for the next guy and his reason for being on that sound stage. He's the key to your technical instrument. He can help you to be very good, or he can sabotage you.

There are many technical-minded people, some brilliant, in the industry who can't get a job. The ones who function best seem to be very human. They might not be as well qualified as the super-technician but they bring a tremendous insight to the material and its projection.

So I maintain we're dealing in a humanities area just as critical, in its way, as open-heart surgery. I don't care how much technical information you have stored away, you blow the picture when you blow the human end. Everything is going for you—beautiful setup, marvelous cast, wonderful sets, crew, et cetera. And then someone says, "Good luck. It's your first day. It's nine o'clock. Make your first shot."

"Wha-wha-wha-wha!"

Here he comes now! Here is Ray Milland and there is Ann Sothern! "Ah, Miss Sothern, I saw you on television and you were pretty shitty. Now, here's your first shot . . ."

Forget it. It's over. Burn the set. Forget it.

"Mr. Milland, you look a little old for this part, but we'll see what we can do."

Out! It's over.

Actors will kill for you if you treat them like human beings. You have to let them know you want them and need them; pay them what they want, but don't overpay them; treat them kindly. Give an actress a clean dress and see that she gets fresh coffee in the mornings, and other little spoon-feedings. She will kill for you.

I once worked for a director who had a personality like Eva Braun's. I was doing a scene, a fall, and told him to forget the stunt man. "I'll fall downstage. You're in a close angle and you're low. It'll be a rough cut for you. I'll do the fall."

"Okay, great!"

I wasn't doing it for him, really. I wanted it to work. Although in the end I suppose I was doing it for him because he'd have to cut the film. So I did it.

"Perfect," he said. "Cut! Print!"

He proceeds to the next setup while I'm cocked down with one leg hanging. The son-of-a-bitch didn't say "Thank you," or even nod his head. Just "Perfect."

He lost me with that one scene, and never got me back. I did my funny faces, and took the money; wished him good luck, and lied about that. I guess I hurt myself, because the comedian on the screen wasn't very funny when the film was released.

Frank Tashlin, on the other hand, was great at handling Jerry Lewis the comic. He has a feeling for people. Very possibly I learned more about the humanities of making films from Frank than I did from everyone else combined. He was a caring director.

I realize that I am basically a miserable bastard on the sound stage. It comes from trying to be a perfectionist. If the toilet seat is left up, I faint.

It's like Queeg and "Who ate the strawberries?"

"Who left the toilet seat up?"

To work for this kind of maniac, you have got to be some kind of dingaling. Yet I get the good dingalings film after film, and the rewards are great. I consciously root for them, and that is what it is all about.

The relations with crew are not much different from the relations with actors. A strong feeling, for good or bad, runs through a crew. They are as adult as I am, and as childish. They like to be "made-over" a bit. You are going to walk by a grip or electrician? What the hell is wrong in recognizing him? I've always done it, not so much for their comfort, but selfishly for mine. I'm more comfortable not having to turn my head away. If I don't know his name, I'll say something: "What right do you have to be working here, you dirty, lousy old . . ."

It is a wild goddamn but very understandable thing. You take a guy who is yawning away, and then suddenly make him special by saying, "How's it going? The first day's tough, right?"

And he answers, "Yeh, but what the hell?"

All of a sudden he's a tiger. "Hey, can I give you a hand here?"

If a grip walks past me and says "Hi," but doesn't add "Jerry," I act offended, and it's not all acting. "Hey, how come I know your name, but you don't know mine. I'm the movie star." It works. I want that personal relationship.

For years I've had a thing in my operation that I call *fear extraction*. The first thing I try to do with a new member of the staff is extract the fear that insecurity, God and Saint Peter handed down. I try to do it simply—tell him that I care, that I don't want to hurt him, that I want him to excel, to be happy. Then I'll be happy making what I love best, film. It works, too.

One night on *The Ladies Man* I had to wrap up a sequence or it would have cost an additional hundred thousand. The crew knocked off at eight o'clock, went to dinner, and then came back to work until three in the morning to finish it. Two days passed before the unit manager told me that the 116 technicians had all punched out at eight o'clock, and had dinner on their own time. They contributed the time between nine P.M. and three the next morning. Had they stayed on the overtime clock, it would have cost something around $50,000.

That's a pretty good example of rapport, and the humanities. It doesn't happen often in this town called Hollywood, but in this new day of making films, it will probably happen more. Everyone will be the better for it. There are other examples, of course. Rossellini fell in love with casts and crews, and told them so. He took trite scripts and developed fine films out of love, and the labor of love. That love magic enters into it big.

The funniest part of creative people, particularly people who love film, is that they get up in the morning and can't wait to run into somebody to hug. A hug does not have to be embracing a male, so that the cops pick you up. A hug is in the voice; a hug is in the spirit; a hug is in the attitude. Kibitz or tease someone to put him down for a second! It only takes another second to let him know it wasn't meant to be unkind. If there isn't rapport and communication, those love magics of film, then the technical information isn't worth a damn.

Hugs, kisses and happy talk don't mean I favor playtime on any set. If there's someone I don't like, I have to let them know why; then see how well I can function with him on a human level. Otherwise, one of us will sabotage.

There will be shmucks midst all the hugging. They take advantage. There is always one who doesn't understand honesty when it is laid on the line. He'll try to undermine. Get rid of him! Save some sabotage. But care must be taken not to let that experience start you off wrong with the replacement. The past screwing has to be forgotten; the humanities pulled in again.

Part of what's wrong with the film industry in America is a couple of goddamn greedy unions and some crew types protected by the unions. But what film-makers, new and old, always have to remember is that there are usually 116 men around who are willing to kill for them. They will gladly assassinate as long as there is rapport.

Humanities go beyond cast and crew rapport. Those who are loving film-makers don't hope another producer's picture will go down the drain. Sam Goldwyn doesn't do that. Louis B. Mayer, who was the murderer of the world in business, didn't do it. Mr. Mayer once told me, "If you don't want that picture I make to be a smash, you're stupid. Your coming attractions might be playing with it."

The people who don't root for another guy's film are the ones who are fearful their own product will bomb. If there can be thirty other film-makers in front of their own demise, it won't be such a bad fall. If they had confidence in their own work, the first thing they'd do is pray for the next guy's work, because he keeps the theaters open.

I could be shooting on a sound stage on Vine Street when a film like *Funny Girl* opens in New York. Should I worry? Absolutely. That theater may fold if *Funny Girl* goes on its ass. Then where will I go with mine? That's healthy thinking. Additionally, I just happen to be a rooter.

But Hollywood is a pretty strange place sometimes. For instance, I took out a full-page ad in a trade paper to congratulate a certain studio for making a certain film, simply because I could take my children to see it. I said, "Bravo for making a good film." But I didn't hear from the producer, didn't hear from the studio. Dead silence for boosting their picture. I had rooted in vain. Now I take the trouble to call attention to what I do. It is no longer a nice thing, but I'm spelling it out in the future.

In contrast to that studio's behavior, I remember going into Abe Schneider's office at Columbia. He runs that studio and is a man of dignity and taste. Very excited, he said, "Look at what *Funny Girl* did!" He should have been excited at the box-office figures. It was a Columbia film. But then he added, "The business is churning. *How the West Was Won*, Metro. Warner-Seven Arts, *Bonnie and Clyde*. Did you ever see figures like that?"

The film-maker who really has the ball park, with the bat and the ball and the ground rules, loses none of his strength or integrity by dealing in humanities on the set as well as throughout the industry. He doesn't have to. If he knows his job, he doesn't need to slam a fist down and yell, "Goddammit, this is the way . . ." It never gets to that, because he is honest with himself, with those around him, and he cares for the product. He'll lick the face of a man who can make an important production contribution.

I suppose what I have been talking about is simple, decent human behavior. But it is the most complex thing around. Some of it can be cut through with a hug and a smile. It is that tangible, intangible basis of it all—the all-meaning relationships with actors, crews, executives and the public.

2

THE TOTAL FILM-MAKER

I have some hates in film—the schmuck who works with it and, deep down doesn't like anything about it; also, the guy who doesn't care how he works. The other-type person I hate is the untotal film-maker who loftily claims he is dealing with the "human magic" of reels, dictating what the emulsion sees and does, and yet has nothing to say. I think he's taking up space. You can automate that kind of film-maker. They come out of a box on a side of a Sperry-Rand thing that says, "I'll make whatever you want."

On the other hand, we don't necessarily have to lay on a tag of importance only when laboring with what we have been told are *the* issues. I buy the premise that we are, as an international whole, responsible film-makers. We tackle an *Advise and Consent* or a *Z*. We must also tackle the comedy of *Dagwood and Blondie* with the same care and a sense of importance, believing that it will make a contribution.

Education is a curse in this respect. The curse on the creative level is that often we have been made to understand that only certain subjects are status subjects; certain themes, valid. Anything else is viewed over the bridge of an intellectual nose and put down. Good Christ, on that basis, how can we remain committed and responsible film-makers if we are making, by choice, subjects that do not fall into those categories?

I'm living proof of the effect of this intellectual snobbery. I cannot sit at certain tables at the Directors' Guild because I make what some people consider is a "hokey" product. John Frankenheimer waves and hopes that no one else sees his hand, simply because I film pratfalls and spritz water and throw pies. But I believe, in my own way, that I say something on film. I'm getting to those who probably don't have the mentality to understand what the hell *A Man for All Seasons* is all about, plus many who did understand it.

I am not ashamed or embarrassed at how seemingly trite or saccharine something in my films will sound. I really do make films for my great-great-grandchildren and not for my fellows at the Screen Directors' Guild or for the critics! I'm never going to meet my great-great-grandchildren in these seventy-some years that may be allotted to me, but when they see my films they'll also see what I wanted to say. And they won't be purposely bad or uncaring films. As a matter of pride, I also hope I look nifty for them.

I believe that the quickest way to find out your capacity for being a *total* film-maker is to determine whether or not you have something to say on film. If the answer is negative, I suggest saving grief and dropping out. Total film-making requires the definite point of view. Of course, an awful lot is *meant* to be said in many films, mine included, that doesn't get across. That's no crime. The crime is starting out by having nothing to say.

As long as he is honest unto himself, I am not going to put anyone down if he just wants to grind footage, function only on a technical level, and make money. There is nothing particularly wrong with that, but it falls beneath the category of total film-making, and should be recognized as such.

The film-maker constantly skates between himself and the audience. Which comes first? Both, hopefully, but it is such a fine line, such an intangible line, that the only way he can proceed is to first please himself. The discipline of the audience is always out there to keep somewhat of a balance. And he cannot presume that the audience will see his film more than once. They will judge it on that first-time basis.

There is no way to put on the table the heartaches, palpitations, dreams and hopes that can't be bought with a check. Yet they aren't things you call upon as a starting director or as one with a hundred film credits. "I, too, shall be that way." You *are* that way, or you aren't. It's the difference between a film-loving, total film-maker, or just a film-maker. Even if you flop, you're better off with your heart in film than if you're just a good mechanic.

In terms of totality, I think a film I am in, and have not directed, is less of a film even though the public may judge it otherwise. Dedication can't be bought with a director's salary. No one can write a check for concern; no one can say to a director, "Here is a hundred thousand, pray for it, love it, take care of it, sit at the moviola all night long and edit us a masterpiece." The price is really based on X number of week's work. If lucky, there may be dedication and concern—maybe only technical function.

When you make a film yourself, write it, produce it, direct it, perhaps star in it; a piece of your heart enters the emulsion. It stays there the rest of your life, good film or bad. So, from a purely personal viewpoint, the film I directed and starred in is a hundred times better than the other man's film starring me, simply because of the care it was given. Going in, the chances of success are better because of that dedication.

Also, as a total film-maker, I'm convinced that there is a greater chance of inconsistency when the four separate minds of writer, producer, director and actor collaborate. I know about spreading one's self too thin—I've lived with it year after year—but care is the antitoxin to a thin-spread project.

I want to see four different men make the "Mona Lisa"; four men sculpt something elegant, four men make a baby. That's my answer to anyone who hits me with the idea that committees, three or four central minds, make the best films. They often make good films, rarely the best.

A one-man film effort at least has the potential of being a "Mona Lisa." *Monsieur Verdoux* was not accepted as a fine film, nor was *Limelight,* but both had the potential of being Chaplin's "Mona Lisa." They failed. Even so, they were better by far than the majority of committee films.

A man who is going to write, produce, direct and act in a film argues more with himself, fights a greater battle than any battle with all the other bright committee minds choosing to give him static. The battle within himself is part and parcel of what makes him a total film-maker. He struggles within one mind. One hat fights the other. Often the actor cannot stand what the director says. The producer thinks the director is a moron. And the writer is disturbed by all three of them. The total film-maker cannot lie to any of his separate parts and be successful. There is a tremendous inner government within him, and his judgment is severely examined by that inner government.

The committee way, it's always, "Well, who'll tell him?" The committee way, you can walk away from the director. Or when you wrap the set at six o'clock, saying, "I'll argue with you tomorrow, Mr. Star." The one-man total way, you must eat and sleep with it. You don't win arguments because you want to win them.

Some film-makers can never be multifaceted simply because they cannot be that objective. It isn't something you buy in a store: "Give me three pounds of objectivity, please." You have it, or you don't.

For example, the director-writer hat does not always help the multifaceted film-maker. It depends on the kind of writer he is; depends on the kind of director he is. A lovely thing happens to a director-writer. As the writer, he can easily become the director's enemy. Alternatively, the director can become the enemy because he has placed the writer in traps. However, if you are objective enough while wearing the two hats, you will not blame yourself but blame "the writer" as if he doesn't exist within you.

If you're functioning as director at a given moment, it takes tremendous will power, objectivity and know-how to leave the writer in his office when you are writer-director, to leave the producer in his office when you are producer-director. Yet it can be done. It's even rougher as director-actor when you sit back in dailies and turn to the cutter, "Dump him. He isn't funny. I did something wrong with him." Total film-makers are usually objective enough to know what they want, what they did right; to admit what is wrong. Objectivity will indicate when the film is running away on its own.

In my case, if I believe the character up there on the screen is funny I'll laugh at him. There are no egos or vanities if he isn't. They are kept in the desk drawer. Egos and vanities do come out when you dress up like a movie star and watch yourself on the screen. Sitting in the projection room, looking at the bread and butter, you become a slasher. No one on that screen has value if he is getting in the way. Objectivity has no relatives.

The total film-maker bears the sometimes expensive curse of never being really satisfied. He can approach but never gain it. He is driven to this by being rather totally identified with his product. So, he must strive for self-satisfaction.

I've spent an extra half million dollars on a film because of this curse. Truthfully, the film wasn't improved that much but I had seen mistakes which I thought should be corrected. The comedian I'd cast and directed wasn't funny. Whatever pressures were on him, and why he wasn't funny, were not of importance. He'd failed. I re-shot his part simply because I wasn't satisfied.

Of course, many times a director's design and intention becomes something other than what it was meant to be. He will lose control of the film if he loses objectivity. It will tend to travel its own course in that literal sense. Occasionally, this is salvation. Mostly, it is disaster. Yet all directors, good or bad, will sometimes accept exactly what the film gives them.

In my own experience, I've gotten some things I really didn't intend and found myself accepting them. I could not decide how much was me, and how much was the magic and emulsion mystery. This happens.

Another aspect of the film-maker's objectivity is the practical application to "different." Suddenly, miraculously, he thinks he has done something entirely new. After a while, he stops lying to himself, applies objectivity and gets around to the realization that some pretty good minds have passed along the same route. His "different," or switch on past work, remains valid but he sees it in its true light.

It's hell being objective. I've had more retakes on Jerry Lewis than anyone else in the production. I use video tape, shot simultaneously, for instant viewing of any scene. The video camera monitors every take. But I never view the tape except when I'm in doubt. One advantage I've had is playing night clubs, theaters and concerts. I do ninety minutes performing in Las Vegas making audiences laugh. Timing tells me what to do and how. If it's working, I don't need the audience to tell me. It is right because it *feels* right. The same applies to the sound stage. I view the video for mistakes. At that moment, all the objective hyphenated hats are functioning.

Yet it is often torture when you have complete personal control. You answer to yourself once you get it. The pain is justified when you answer to a bunch of stupid front-office morons. Eventually, you may beg not to have autonomy so that the morons can pass judgment. You can lie back and bleed, whimpering safely, "Look what they did to me."

Autonomy in film, as well as in any other endeavor, is always a tough rap because it basically deals with your own integrity. There is no easy way to shake that schmuck you sleep with at night. No matter how you toss and turn, he's always there.

I have to sleep with that miserable bastard all the time. Very painful, sometimes terrifying.

A good film-maker must have the guts to quit. If somebody challenges what he says, or denies him the right to believe what he has said, he must fight back, spit it out, and if necessary, walk out. Total film-making cannot be approached on the basis of compromise.

Autonomy, if you are lucky enough to be the producer, writer and director, cuts away a lot of the fat but spreads the hours. One beleaguered morning you wake up to ask, "How does the director, who is a total film-maker, put in twenty-one needed hours in a working day?"

Well, on a nine-to-six basis on the stage, you eat up three in camera setups, which leaves six. One for lunch leaves you five. Of those five, you talk to actors for two while rehearsing and waiting for the lighting. Another hour, perhaps, is spent talking to the crew. Before you know it, you have two hours of actual shooting time to pick up three minutes of screen time.

What's happened to the other twelve hours? Somehow, they sandwich in. In that nine-hour day at the studio or on location, you're involved in wardrobe, building or striking of sets, casting, script, dailies, publicity, money and a supporting player's hay fever. Even if you were only hired as a director, and not a *hyphenate*—a producer-director or writer-director—you'd still be dealing in most of these areas.

Unfortunately the film-maker cannot design a specific sequence and deal just with the actors, the script and camera movement. The design often involves the unexpected. The set scheduled for the afternoon's work suddenly vanishes. The unit production manager, the nuts-and-bolts foreman of the entire operation, coughs, "Jeez, they just told me it's not ready."

So the homework of last night is so much scrap paper now. You have to do another scene, possibly one you haven't really prepared. (Actually, you do nightly homework on what has been prepared for months but bone up specifically for the next day's work.) The total film-maker, knowing all parts of his operation, develops an elasticity that helps in emergencies.

Even without the producer or writer roles tossed in, the dimensions of the director's work alone are sometimes frightening. There is no such thing as being "just a director" in today's industry. When D. W. Griffith walked on the set years ago, everything was laid out for him. Today, even the key departments of a decade ago are ghosts. It is now the director's bag and he must be somewhat multifaceted even though he does not produce or write.

Whatever I am as a producer-writer in this total category, I am a hard-ass director. Otto Preminger was a hard-ass director before anyone knew that Preminger wasn't a skin disease. A hard-ass director arrives at his iron nates by knowing his craft. Few can get to him. That is where sound stage strength lies.

I've found that when you know your racket, you can't sleep a full eight hours. You want to work; can't wait to get your hands on the goddamn film. The strength is already there and comes from information. Oddly, yet understandably, the stronger you are in all the know-hows to make a total film, the more tender you seem when it comes to the cast and crew humanities on the set. Security versus insecurity.

Beyond that strength it turns back to the individual director and what *he is;* what he has to say, hard-ass or not. Karl Menninger once remarked, "The psychiatrist is not good because of what he has learned and what he knows by way of texts. He is good because of what he is." It applies to directing films.

I think total film-making has always been misunderstood by the Hollywood onlookers. They presume it is little less than purest egomania. I don't buy that. I simply don't want anyone tampering with what I believe.

I want to make a piece of crap. If it is a piece of crap, let it be mine. Don't add and join. My crap and your crap do not meld. Let mine be good crap by itself.

And the only way to retain full control over your piece of crap is to hold the reins yourself by being a total film-maker.

3

THE MONEY MAN

I had a notion to write a film about a crazy bellboy. I'd toyed with the idea quite a while but didn't tackle it until another completed film ran into a release-date problem. Unable to get the desired booking date for it, I still needed product in the theaters. So I grabbed the hotel story.

I planned pantomime for the star's role, a pretty wild device for a feature, and knew that would rattle the studio executives. It rattled me a little, too, and I knew I'd be lucky if it worked. However, I had enough faith in it to put up a million and a quarter of my own money. That is a fair amount of faith.

It took eight days to write *The Bellboy* and I also wore

the hats of producer, director and star. I decided to make it in black and white, the quickest, cheapest way, simply because of the push for the theaters. It went okay, and I shot it in Miami. It took five weeks.

Then, at the sneak preview, the studio executives began to tell me what was wrong. They turn into experts at previews. Naturally, they were preconditioned against it because of the pantomime. More than that, they were in a part of the theater where they couldn't plainly hear all the laughs. They concluded I had a bomb and buried me like crazy with all kinds of suggestions.

I listened carefully and made notes like a good producer. Then I took the picture back into the cutting room. I let them think we were slaving for a day and a half. Actually, we never opened a can for deletions. We previewed again three nights later. They smiled, "Now, Jer, you've got a picture." We hadn't made a cut. We had made a slight addition.

The execs had been concerned that the audience wouldn't understand why there was no plot. So I shot a piece of film opening on a supposed exec of the studio. His narration was, "The picture you are about to see relates to nothing. It is a series of silly sequences. There's no plot, no story. And, it's just silly." He gets hysterical with laughter, swings around in his leather swivel chair; then yells to the projectionist, "Put it on!"

I made him a real dingaling, a stereotype of a studio executive. They loved that. It made the picture for them.

And they thought all their suggested cuts had been made. One said, "Gee, that's marvelous. What a difference!"

The Bellboy grossed $6 million (and is still earning dollars) which I shared with the studio. To this day, some of these executives honestly believe the film was re-cut. They "saved" it for me.

That experience is an example of producer function, both in quickly putting together a film for a specific need, and also in resisting changes that are considered questionable. One way or another, you must sleep with the studio executives if you are in partnership with them.

This whole thing about previews, or sneaking the picture, is a circus unto itself. An audience preview tells the producer and director what works, what doesn't; what is thin, fat; needs pace, or needs cutting. You may know all the answers before you go in, or you may think you know them, but it is surprising to see the picture play before a cross section.

Many people in attendance think they are vitally important because of what they write on the reaction cards. Actually, their spontaneous reactions to the film—laughing, crying, belting the guy next to them, or sitting like dummies—are the guides to how it plays.

Once I made a film solely as a producer, although I had to finish it as a co-director because of chaff on the set. Nothing ever runs smoothly. Anyway, my money was in it and I cared beyond the money. The preview was set for November 29, and the studio provided me with a list of eleven available theaters and films playing in them: *The Brotherhood, Candy*, and everything else, from *Rabbi Magnin Converts* to *Ma And Pa Kettle Have Hysterectomies*. There were some doozies. Only eleven theaters in the area had a dual system enabling the running of the separate film and sound tracks. You usually do not go to the *composite*, or marriage of the film and sound, until after you've previewed. Changes are costly if you are in *composite*.

"Strike the twenty-ninth of November. Check me out for next week. Give me the runs," I said to Rusty Wiles, who is my long-time film editor.

Care must be taken in the selection of a theater. A western should not be previewed in a theater playing a slick bedroom comedy, nor a murder film with a Walt Disney production. The wrong audience will be in the house. I looked at Rusty's list of runs: *Brotherhood*'s in theaters for three weeks firm. That's the only way the distribution company would sell it—70 percent to them, and 30 to the theaters. I'm dead in that theater, which leaves me ten houses. San Diego has *The Odd Couple*. Good movie, family show. Okay, Rusty, let's get it.

But what? It's in the third week. They've only got enough people in San Diego to play a full house for that one for ten days. So I could be sneaking my picture to a cat and an usher. Next week, then.

Next week went into the following week, and Christmas passed. Then they blew the horns for New Year's. Finally, in early January, I said, "We'll go to San Diego and I don't care what it's playing with."

We previewed January 11 and it was the best preview I'd had in thirty-eight films. The place was loaded with derelicts. Whole bananas, not just the peels, were in the aisles. Sensational!

But I'd lost the time since November 29. I was against the gun if I didn't get to the moviola for any changes on a post-dubbing session, or polish, on January 13—I wouldn't make the Easter release. If I didn't make it, I would be locked out of distribution in the domestic United States for one helluva long time.

I had two million three hundred thousand in this film and other product commitments for two years ahead. Without the Easter release I had nowhere to go with it. Sure, sell it to television. Lose a million eight. Not this producer!

There is a system called blind bidding. Once the producer announces he has product that will be available, he can silently sell and book for the release. But if it isn't ready at the stated time, the theaters will move on with other product. He is locked out for months ahead. MGM or Warner–Seven Arts might move in. United Artists or independents like Joe Levine will take the theaters. So dates are highly critical and the producer respects his schedule.

I made the Easter date, panting right down to the wire. The game is called MONEY.

❂   ❂   ❂

Most times a producer puts the financial pieces together and then drops the responsibility of making the film into the hands of the director. Producers vary in functions, muscle and ability, but the ones deserving of their titles have more to do than play golf. Good ones beat the director through the studio gates in the morning. But in this changing Hollywood the producer, functioning in that capacity alone, has fewer creative responsibilities. The director is pushing him off the lots.

There was a time, of course, when Hollywood producers could play God as well as Saint Peter. Actors bowed to them and directors sent them golf balls. One of the first producers I worked for was a marvelous human being on a personal level, but behind his desk he was the original Jekyll and Hyde. A wild man with a fantastic capacity for being unkind, he was usually so busy attacking the people on his payroll that he lost some degree of concentration.

It took me a while to learn how to cope with him. At first, I'd go to his office and say, "This sequence is crap. I don't know why you want it in the picture." He'd answer, "Rewrite it."

"You don't pay me as a writer. You want me to write for nothing?"

"Then do the crap," he'd say.

"But it's terrible. It's going to hurt your picture."

"OK. Rewrite it."

I'd yell, "You don't pay me as a writer."

"Then, do what's on the paper."

So the night before we'd shoot I'd do a complete revision. For free!

On the same picture I went to him with an idea. I said, "I got something marvelous. If we can get the kid to want to really be like his father, work in front of a mirror . . ."

"No," he answered, "I like it the way it is. Screw off."

I screwed off but I'd begun to learn. I loved that picture and didn't want anything to louse it up. Three days later I went back to his office. I said, "You know that idea *you* told the director about the kid, and his father . . . the mirror. That's the best thing I ever heard."

He said, "You like it?"

We did it! What's more, the son-of-a-bitch really thought it was his idea. I worked that routine at least a dozen times with him.

"Remember that night when we were having a drink at Lucey's and you said the girl shouldn't dance? That was very smart."

"Yeah?"

He couldn't wait to get the broad out of the picture!

She was out, out, out! It was *his* idea.

When I finished my contract, I wrote him a note: "Thank you for putting me in the picture business but please don't confuse my gratitude with my principles. You are a shit."

A film producer is dealing in big dollar business. If he

has a hot property and a hot concept, he can wheel and deal. If his product is worth anything to the studios and they like his talent, he can make almost any deal he wants within the economics of a given year. That won't last, however, past one or two pictures if he isn't successful. Success, naturally, instant or otherwise, gives him a "track record" for future deals. Continued success will bring backing from outside, non-studio sources.

The amount of studio control, influence or interference with the project is solely dependent on the deal that is made "in front," long before the film starts. Under my former Paramount partnership I had to answer to that studio 50 percent of the time. Then I decided it wasn't worth it, became a full independent, and now sell my product to a "distributor's seal." It could be Paramount, Columbia, Metro, or any other releasing company.

When the film-maker is working on a completely independent basis, the studio is actually working for him. He can buy their seal, whether it's Leo the lion or the Paramount mountain, and their distribution costs thirty-three and a third of your profits. He may have a partnership relationship with them, retaining two-thirds' control of his picture. It can be another arrangement, with varying percentages, but until the studio obtains 51 percent he still has control.

Usually the studios charge 32.5 against the picture as overhead, compensation for using their sound stages and facilities. That figure can vary, too. If the film-maker brings in a best seller, Marlon Brando and a key director, the overhead charge may drop to 20 percent. They seldom budge on distribution fees. But where else does the independent go? The studios have worldwide distribution organizations which advertise and publicize, then sell the films to the theaters.

Once I have the general terms spelled out—my production company will make a picture for X number of dollars, so many dollars for the release—the attorneys on both sides go to work on the contract's fine print and I go forward with the production.

As with all businesses the largest single problem is financing. In 1970 it is becoming almost prohibitive to make a film. I think the greatest contributing factors to the problem are unions and feather-bedding practices. I hold thirteen union cards and have a positive feeling toward unions. However, they are committing suicide.

As an example of runaway costs, a certain member of my crew earned $401 per week on a five-day basis during the making of *Hook, Line and Sinker.* Two years previously his salary had been $201 a week, a jump of almost 100 percent in twenty-four months. Additionally, feather-bedding practices have been rampant in the industry for years. Some unions have agreed to alter them. We shall see.

A film made for $1.8 million five years ago now costs $2.7 million. Our total economy has skyrocketed but not that much. Two years ago I could hire a good composer for $7,500. Now I can't touch one for less than $10,500. Because of all the escalated costs, the producer now thinks in terms of a 60 by 40 set instead of a 100 by 80 set. The larger one would add production values to his film, but he can't afford it.

Not long ago I had a meeting with my production staff. They were trying to shuffle dollars. There was a figure of $7,700 to build a set. Yet they told me if I struck the sequence and didn't build the set, I'd only save $80.

I said, "Explain that to me. If I strike the set I should save $7,700. How does that work?"

For three hours I tried to get a plausible explanation. I might as well have been talking to Internal Revenue. They said, "Well, the fringe benefits . . ."

"I want to know more about Mr. Fringe. I want to meet him. I also want to meet Messrs. Pension and Insurance!"

Those three guys are going to wipe us out of business. Mr. Fringe is a goddamn millionaire. Mr. Pension is a billionaire. With all his money, Mr. Insurance should be making pictures.

Now, Miss C! She is Miscellaneous. Miss C! What a bitch! She has more money in the film than I have. The only explanation I ever get is, "Well, it's in Miscellaneous."

I looked at her in budgets until I finally said, "She isn't in my picture any more. How do you like that? Make her someone else. Make her lumber, grip's tools, hammers, nails, wire. But no more Miss C!"

I think she has $3 million of my money and she's living down in South America with Martin Bormann.

I usually pay around $100,000 for a script. To the layman that may be a staggering sum, but if the picture is successful it is relatively the lowest cost of the production. If I write the screenplay myself, as I did in *Bellboy*, I am still working for my company and have to be paid like anyone else. I either take the money, accepting the dollars in a certain period, or put it into the corporation and defer. I do take the money *now* as an actor. Want me to work in your movie, pay me! Other phases I can defer because I can't afford myself, silly as that may sound. Tax governs deferments and acceptances. These are all considerations of the producer.

A larger and related consideration is profit and loss. Years ago the ratio of negative cost of the film to profit was two to one. Then it climbed two and a half to one. Now, it is three to one. A $3 million film must get back $9 million before a nickel of profit is seen. It isn't the production cost alone. Theater-owner profits, distribution fees, cost of exhibition prints and publicity men's luncheons are lumped in.

Then the firing squad lurks beyond the hangman's noose. Taxes—federal, state, interstate, county, city! Someone will claim space and tax the Telstar bounce! There is a $50,000 California state tax slapped on the negative. If a film is started in November 1970 and bleeds into April of 1971, there's another fifty thousand in surtax. Getting the negative out of the state prior to March 15 saves fifty thousand. However, if the film is started in April and then completed, with negative shipped, before the end of the calendar year, the original fifty thousand is saved. A lot of studios ship to New York and cut negative there to save the tax bite.

In the bracket of an independent film-maker, who also happens to be the star and has a corporate setup, the dollars are ten to one. When I spend a dollar I have to earn ten within that structure. If I can save fifty thousand by cutting in New York, I have actually saved a half million. These are also producer considerations.

Cutting costs is the producer's job, but he cannot cut three to one. Having your own staff and crew picture after picture helps tremendously. I think you can take a two-million-two production and bring it in at a million eight with that crew that works regularly with you, for you, and cares enough. That is back to the humanities of making film. They can put in an eight-hour day in four, or an eight in eight. If they don't happen to like you, or your premise, chances are you'll get eight hours in eight hours.

The producer-and-director relationship is more vital today than ever, but it is also slowly becoming dual throughout the industry, simply because of the thrust of business. The producer's questions were usually the ones the director would have to answer anyway. That is why creators like Stanley Kramer decided to combine the job, going from his former role of producer to both producer and director. He found he could save time and static. The same applies to

Otto Preminger, Billy Wilder and Joe Mankiewicz. To me!

After assuming the dual role, Kramer said he was having difficulty maintaining objectivity. I can sympathize. As a one-hat producer, I say to the director, "I'm putting two million four in this picture. Not a dime more. I haven't got it. If you go over that budget, you are responsible for the overage." Midway through the film I see that something is taking shape; I'm tempted to pump in another hundred thousand to give the picture some air, help it along. As strictly a money man, I'm a jerk to give another quarter. As a dual, a producer-director, I may think otherwise.

I function with an associate producer on all my films. He minds the bankroll, does follow-ups and handles details. He looks over my shoulder so that I don't sign an actor for twelve weeks when I only need him eight.

He becomes involved in the "mind fights." On the sound stage, I might say, "I told you to get me five hundred calves and three thousand black girls with fourteen Jews." He replies, "Christ, those fourteen Jews are really going to cost us. Why not two hundred calves less?"

As the director, I answer, "Exactly what I said, and no less."

Early next morning in my producer's office, an hour away from shooting, I might turn to him: "What do we need with five hundred calves? Knock off two hundred."

The producer-and-director relationship should be completely give and take. On *One More Time* I occupied the director's chair, happily doffing the producer's hat, as well as that of writer and star. The producer of the film saw his responsibilities primarily as financial ones.

Early in the film he came to me to say, "I won't bother you on the set."

"Hold it a moment," I remember saying. "When you come on my set it is yours . . . until you want to take it over. Then I'll remind you it's mine."

I told him that when he was looking at dailies and felt the need for another piece of film—a close-up or whatever, no matter his reason—he should make it known.

He replied, "I'll never do that unless I think it's absolutely necessary."

I could not buy that, either. In many cases, the director will miss something that the producer has in mind. The two roles should not have strict boundaries. I answered, "I want you to do it. I'll deliver the additional piece of film but I shoot the new material."

When you're working solely as a director you have to adjust, function the way you expect your crew to function. However, it is difficult for a director to face an overpowering producer. The best way to beat those elephants is to see that the actors say the words. He has lived with the script; he knows what he wants to hear. Strangely, you can get away with theft optically if you let the producer hear on screen what he's already read a hundred times.

We made *One More Time* in England, which is still another example of producer involvement. Where do you make the picture? Can you cut costs by making it on foreign soil? In this case, we did, by utilizing the Eady Plan. Under it, and by using an all-British crew and staff except for three Americans, we gained an extra percentage of the profits accruing in England and its possessions.

But generally the boom is out of making films overseas. A picture that formerly cost nine hundred thousand in Italy has climbed to a million seven now. Often, production problems on overseas locations far outweigh the financial benefits. Producers take jets principally to escape unions. Their story could be made just as well in Fresno.

There is a trend back toward low-budget films in America simply because the studios are up against the financial wall as the result of spiraling costs and in some cases bad management. But true low-budget films cannot be made in the studios. Massive overheads and union costs make even low-budget films relatively expensive. A million-dollar project is now a low-budget film.

In this day the producer who can get true value out of his production dollar is a genius. And like good directors, good producers are rare. In fact, they are becoming extinct.

4

SCRIPT AND WRITER

Over the years, Hollywood has purchased some marvelous material and then destroyed it on films. You wonder why? I think one reason is that we have a number of creative frauds who convert material to suit their own beliefs because of their own egos. What finally appears on the screen in no way represents the book. They defend their conversions with nonsense about "inner workings" and "the subconscious." Most of it is Freudian garbage.

So it is rare to see a good book rise above itself on film. It only happens when the director and screenplay writer respect and fully understand what the novelist had to say. And their true function is to project, in cinematic form, the ideas of the original material. They should be capable of rising above it without reconstructing it or changing the ideas. At its very best, film will add dimensions to the original story because of animation and the many cinematic devices the director can employ.

Finding good properties to film is similar to mining 100-carat diamonds. They don't come along often. When they do, bidding is high. Even good original screenplays are comparatively scarce. Every studio and independent company is on a constant search for suitable material, and despite the thousands of submissions each year only a few are bought. Of those, only one or two are really outstanding.

I have been in the throes of trying to buy *The Catcher in the Rye* for a long time. What's the problem? The author, J. D. Salinger! He doesn't want more money. He just doesn't even want to discuss it. I'm not the only Beverly Hills resident who'd like to purchase Salinger's novel. Dozens have tried. This happens now and then. Authors usually turn their backs on Hollywood gold only because of the potential for destruction of their material. I respect them for it!

Why do I want it? I think I'm the Jewish Holden Caulfield. I'd love to play it! That's why actors buy any property. Producers and directors buy a property because they like the story. Actors buy it because they see themselves in a part.

I buy it for all those reasons. Additionally, Salinger and I had similar backgrounds and there is empathy. Yet I'm not sure that *Catcher in the Rye* will work with an older guy. So, if age gets in the way, I'll find a young one.

Another aspect of buying a property like this is the opportunity to work with an author of Salinger's ability. With a Salinger, projects open up; with a Salinger, you kill to retain the basic material. So I'll keep trying to buy his story.

The work of the director and the writer should be a fruitful if not always happy marriage. One cannot function without the other. But without denying the director his rightful place, I think the writer has the tougher of the two roles. It is relatively easier to get it on the screen if the script is good, even with production or cast problems. At the same time, it is seldom that a good director can save a bad script. He can help it, but not save it. Conversely, he can take a good script and ruin it, perhaps because of forcing too many of his own ideas into it, or because of a technical lack. Yet the really good script is like a well-made building. It is difficult to destroy completely. It all begins with the writer.

The director must respect the material. If he doesn't respect it, he should have the guts to decline the picture. Without respect for it, his chances of success with it are few. Better he eats hamburgers at Bob's Big Boy for a while than do the script that he inwardly detests.

My greatest worry in tackling a script I did not write is interpretation. I want to be certain that my interpretation of a scene is what the writer had in mind. Usually it is self-evident, but often the words or tone of a scene bring questions. I frequently sit down with my writers for no other reason than to say: It reads this way with me, and this is my approach. Is that right? Is that what you had in mind?

How many changes are made in the screenplay depends on the material, depends on whether it is pre-production, the first day of shooting or the twelfth day. And how well the film is going. If it is the first day, and you've already ironed out most of the difficulties, there is not much reason for surgery or repair. But by the twelfth day, when you have seen film cut together, there may well be reasons for script changes. You have opened some scenes wider, have deleted some, have risen above the script in some areas, and things are not working exactly as planned during preparation.

As an example, I often got script material that is written like a blueprint. It's a visual piece and is really funny but does not tell a hell of a lot. Then the graphic artists go to work on it, using their imagination, and may go off the beaten track. I pull them back. Sometimes they go off the beaten track and it's great. "Hey, that's better!"

Even reading a script is difficult. Few people in the cast and crew read it the same way. The actor often reads his part, and not much else. A property master will read his own ideas into the script. His ideas have nothing to do with wardrobe or the art department. If you leave it up to them and don't have a captain, the director, you are suddenly making eleven different pictures. You're yelling,

"Hey, what did you read?" So the director has to set the tone and communicate that approach to everyone.

Directors have always been accused of rewriting unnecessarily—particularly by writers. Actually, most of the time it is deletion because a scene won't work. You loved it in the original script, okayed it during pre-production, but when you get to the top of the second page of the scene you suddenly discover there is a resolution. It wasn't evident until you took it in front of the camera. Oops, that's the scene! There is no point in mucking up what is already good.

I have collaborated in most of my screenplays and have written nine. When I am working with another writer, my greatest contribution, I think, is a clearer technical basis for shooting. It makes my homework, the preparation, a little less difficult. I try very hard to stick with the other man's material, discipline myself, and invent only when necessary.

Most directors do not want to rewrite the script. They have more pressing commitments on the sound stage. The writer's best insurance against rewrite is to have an understanding of the directorial problems. Writing a scene that can't be played, no matter how beautiful the words or thoughts, is begging for a revamp.

Some writers work in master scene formats. The word *camera* or suggestions on how to use the camera does not appear in the script. They write a play for screen use. Others belabor their scripts with endless descriptions and camera placement to the point where the visual aspect blurs the basic story. I'm more interested in the purpose of the scene. Never mind the camera.

I tell new writers to study old scripts. Dig up a copy of *On the Waterfront*. Or more recently, *In the Heat of the Night* or *The Russians Are Coming, The Russians Are Coming*. These are scripts that needed little revamp on the director's part.

I have found that the best scripts are written, rewritten, and written again before they ever reach the sound stage. The director and writer have married to the point that chopping or adding isn't an everyday occurrence once shooting begins.

There are directors who are not qualified to work over a script; some are not even capable of reading a scene and understanding it. When they begin revamping, it usually results in a trade-paper announcement that the writer would like to have his name taken off the credits. It is difficult to blame him.

The late Ben Hecht, Abby Mann, Sterling Silliphant, Reginald Rose and Isobel Lennart are my ideas of heavyweights in screen writing. But there are many others as talented and as expert.

On my films, those written by someone else, the writer stays with the company until the project is finished. He is constantly called upon for suggestions and contributions. He is not stuck in the cellar.

Titles? Who knows? *The Catcher in the Rye* is a terrific

title only because it is pre-sold. It was a best-selling book and almost a bible in colleges. *West Side Story* was a good film title only because it was a hit musical. *The Bellboy,* with no pre-sold action, was a good title simply because it said in one word what the picture was about.

For the sequel to *Salt And Pepper,* the second Lawford-Davis picture I directed, the distributors, United Artists, were fighting for a title. I finally came up with *The Second Salt And Pepper.*

They said, "Gee, that's pretty simple."

I said, "Yeh. What else do you want to call it? It is the second one."

"Yeh. Well, call it that."

"Okay, yeh."

But who knows about titles? At the last minute the distributors changed the title to *One More Time.*

5

ACTORS

Before the deal is set, while the attorneys squabble endlessly, maybe before a word of script is written, and long before the sets are built, before wardrobe is selected, you're thinking about cast, a specific type of actor for each lead role—later on, the character bits.

I go through the Screen Actors' Guild book section by section, picking the range of faces; then go about picking the people out of that range by age, type and style. I seldom look at film of actors or actresses. I've never looked at film to cast someone in a picture unless the slate, telling me when it was shot and who directed it, is at the head of it. The test tells little without that information.

Every director has his own method, but mine is to have an interview of at least ten minutes. I'm not looking for them to perform. Rather, I want to know *how I feel* when I'm with them. I never ask a performer to read lines during an interview. What does it mean? Reading lines in front of one man in an office is like asking a comedian to do a sketch with a chambermaid. Office performances tell very little.

I'll give screen tests if I'm interested enough. If they are young and new, I want to see what happens when they are in the arena. I also test for make-up, wardrobe or for specific reasons such as optics. These tests, however, usually come after I've made the selection.

Recently I went through the casting routine with a young actress. A moment after she sat down, I asked, "Do you know anything about our story?" It was a rush casting and we hadn't told her agents about the nature of the film.

"No, but I really don't have to know if I'm right for the part."

I answered, "You're not right for this film. I just decided not to use any women. Thank you very much. Goodbye."

I was that quick with her. She'd turned me so goddamn cold. Turned me right off. To her, obviously, it was just a job.

Another girl came in. Jean Shrimpton's sister, Chrissy. Want to see an angel face with a pair of warm eyes? Chrissy has them. She captured my ear, my heart, my eyes! She gave a damn, and I saw her in the part. Maybe a little too young, I thought. But in other clothes? The interview should have lasted ten minutes. Forty-five went by, with other girls stacking up in the outer office. We talked about dozens of things. I felt *right* with her.

I suppose it boils down to personally liking them. That's a fault but that's how it is. If the girl that I'm about to choose as leading lady drops a few words: "I think we should bomb Pasadena . . ." Goodbye, again. There are directors who can live with them. I can't. Occasionally you get a Shirley Temple in the office and a Vampira on the set. You try to say adios once again if you can.

Chaplin, in his autobiography, said that he did not really like actors. Alfred Hitchcock has said the same thing about them, but Hitch is completely different from any other contemporary film-maker. A diabolical old bastard, making no bones about what he has to do for results—I'd make book that his statement was mainly for quoting, part of a plan to create hostility within an actor. Chaplin could never have worked with actors, to his degree of success, without liking them.

I rate them by height and other physical statistics. Height is very important in some pictures. In *Salt and Pepper* No. 2 I had to deal with the difference in size between Sammy Davis, Jr., and Peter Lawford. I've been dearly in love with Sammy for twenty years, but never looked at him in terms of height. His talent is so giant you don't think of size. Suddenly I was aware that Sammy is a tiny man. Maybe five two, five three.

In terms of casting him with a girl, I could easily adjust. She could be several inches taller but adjustment could be made with the camera, with placing them and with movement. But then I was endangering Peter Lawford, a six-footer, perhaps distorting him. There was also his leading lady to think about. Finally I worked it out by placement and camera movement. Disparity in height presents many difficulties.

Ability, personality, name value for a particular part, style, height, weight, looks and the probability of rapport with the director all enter into casting any role. It's one of the more fascinating parts of film-making.

Actors are a strange breed of people. They are all nine years old. They stop at nine. If you want to attempt to understand actors, read a quote from Moss Hart's *Act One*: "The theatre is an inevitable refuge of the unhappy child, and the tantrums and childishness of theatre people are not either accidental nor a necessary weapon of their profession. It has nothing to do with so-called 'artistic temperament.' The explanation, I think, is a far simpler one. For the most part, they are impaled in childhood like a fly in amber."

Locked like flies in their million-year-old amber, they are all different, wearing different costumes, giving different portrayals at different times, yet basically they are all alike—nine-year-old children.

Speaking now as an actor: tremendous ego is involved and we tend to believe that whatever weaknesses we have are justification for our neuroses. That's childlike. If the actor were truly adult, in that strict sense of definition, he could not act. He's standing up there because of *needs*. He must express himself, be heard.

A director, whether he's a Wyler or a student film-maker, cannot run on to the set and yell, "Hey, watch me, I'm going to show off." That is what actors do. That is the actor's need. He's built that way.

But there's a contradiction, too. Once he is on the set telling everyone to watch him, he might also yell, "Close the set." They are there so that everyone in the world can watch them, yet at the same time no one should be permitted to see them act. Very complex people. Actors and directors sometimes close sets to the public because of the complexity of the scene. More often, they do it because of whim and their own complexities.

They are so like children. If they see the director talking to a crew member, momentarily ignoring them, they may pout. In the next scene, they won't even listen. Once they close their ears for whatever reason, whatever puckered petulance, the director may not be able to open them up for a long time. Suddenly he is three days behind schedule. He has, simply but nightmarishly, a case of a pouting actor.

Actors are usually waiting for someone *not to like them.* If the director doesn't let them know where he stands and what he feels, they sometimes interpret it as a disguise for dislike. Most do not have the capacity to say, "He's young and inexperienced and has a problem." The problem is communication. They see it as dislike. Generally, actors "rear-view" everything. They see only what they believe they have motivated.

At the start of one film I tried to look in the mirror at Jerry Lewis the actor. The director was Jerry Paris and we were talking in my office. He asked, "Is there anything I can do to help the film?"

I answered, "If I was directing I wouldn't take any crap from the actors. I wouldn't put up with petulance. At the same time I'd spoon-feed; do the things that are necessary. But I wouldn't give up my dignity and allow them to shit on me. So, now you're going to be dealing with a petulant goddamn actor."

I started to explain the difference between The Kid, The Idiot, my characters, and me. He didn't quite hear. A week later he came over to say, "You are the most petulant, ornery son-of-a-bitch I've ever worked with."

I reminded him, "I told you I was an actor. My call tomorrow morning is nine. I may come in at nine-thirty. I'm doing everything I wouldn't allow an actor to do."

The minute he said it was okay to be late, I changed tactics. The next morning I was on the set an hour before he was. When the crew came in at seven-thirty and asked why I was so early, I replied, "Because the director said I could be late."

Paris then understood about actors.

A few days later he wanted to do something that I thought was wrong. I said, "I feel uncomfortable."

Paris said, "Get your ass in there and do it."

I did it. As I reflect on that film, I wanted nothing more than strength from my director. I already knew he was very human; then I found his strength.

Of late, I'm getting to the point where my needs are lessened. That comes from maturity, possibly peace of mind. I don't know. I really don't have to get up in front of an audience as much now for the plasma of it. I do it now because I really enjoy it and it's fun. The hunger, the need, isn't there any more. I do love to act, however. Why? There is a tremendous satisfaction in making people laugh. It feels good.

Sometimes the neurotic needs of an actor cause problems. By continually being late, Marilyn Monroe is said to have cost 20th Century–Fox $200,000 on *Let's Make Love.* You hear a lot about that cost but very little about the reported $400,000 loss the sound department brought about through use of inferior generators. They were out of synchronization for three numbers of that film. They had to be re-shot. Over the years, staff and crew louse-ups plus antiquated equipment have cost the industry much more than any player's neurotic or unprofessional behavior.

Any actor has his bad days. Directing Vince Edwards in a *Ben Casey* I requested that he read offstage lines to cue an actor. He answered, "I'll be in my dressing room. Have the script girl read them."

I said, "You walk off this set, and you'll stay off." Even

though Vince owned part of the show, the director has to have control, or he won't last the day.

Edwards started walking.

I called after him, "I'm surprised at you, Vince. You're a director as well as an actor. If you don't take my instructions, then you can't come back on the set."

He kept walking.

I told the assistant director, "Keep Vince off the stage," then called the studio police to order the set be closed to him. After fifteen minutes I realized that wasn't enough. I called the producer to say, "If he's allowed on the lot, I won't finish your film. You've got two days to shoot." They barred him. I had a product to finish and I wasn't going to let anyone stand in my way, even one of the owners of the show.

A month later Vince wrote a letter of apology, saying that he'd been wrong. As I look back, Vince did not mean to be unprofessional, but after five years of that mental and physical grind he was entitled to a bad day. He's a nice guy and a fine actor.

Many actors circle only their parts. Nine times out of ten that is all they've read. They don't know who else is in the picture or why. Real professionals learn the whole script, almost know it cue by cue, all of the parts. They circle theirs constructively. That approach was used years ago on the old Jewish stage. The actors, the forerunners of great theater, knew all the roles. It helped them know their own.

Starring actors like Burt Lancaster, Kirk Douglas, Sidney Poitier, Rod Steiger, Cary Grant and Jimmy Stewart learn all the parts. Fine character actors, like Harold J. Stone, know the star's part as well as their own. Jimmy Cagney felt strongly about knowing the other people and how he might improve their roles. In the end, he would be better. He knew that a good actor is a re-actor.

An actor receives solid help when the other actor is good. A bad actor often brings him down to that incompetent level. In vaudeville, years ago, there was an adage, "I'd like to follow the juggler that bombed." Or "Put me on after the fourth singer, the one that does 'Roses are . . .'" Then they learned that was the time the audience would go to the toilet. So they figured it was better to follow World War II, the act that broke up the theater, come out with the audience high and up. Gregory Peck, another caring actor, won't knowingly do a film with an incompetent actor. He knows he'll look almost equally incompetent.

Many actors haven't learned that good makes good, so they resort to techniques like *method*. They don't know how to relate to other actors, so they reach for a crutch. Lee Strasberg teaches method acting and has helped performers simply by "taking them out of themselves." He puts a label on it and charges them. They feel they've picked up additional tools. It is still a crutch.

Sandy Dennis is a method actress. I don't know her but she doesn't do anything for me. I always feel the Strasbergs are in the wings. She doesn't take me with her; she leaves me outside looking in. The director can be blamed, but I have the feeling she can't be steered by a director. Likely she is so strong-willed in her creative output that perhaps she can't be directed. Whatever, I don't get the feeling that she is relating to the other actors.

In an odd way I had trouble relating to control and to myself in *The Nutty Professor*. I had trouble coming out of the character of Buddy Love because I was playing a dirty, lousy bastard. I didn't like him. I didn't even like writing Buddy Love, the despicable, discourteous, uncouth rat, much less playing him. I asked myself: How do I know so well how to be a heel? Was I leaning to a side of me that really existed? Certainly I was. There was truth in him. It was also in me. So I hated him, and couldn't wait to play the alter-character, the nutty professor. Yet I had to relate to both of them and try to play them equally well. The fly in amber!

A great many people in the film industry—actors, actresses and technicians—are without formal training. What school did Paul Muni attend? When he was ten years old he was on roller skates, wearing a big beard, headed for a theater, ready to act twenty minutes later. Edward G. Robinson went to the American Academy for about six months. But that was an entirely different technique of teaching. It was for the theater. Eddie Robinson, Pat O'Brien, Sam Levine, Spencer Tracy—towering names—did plays. That was their training. Cary Grant,

Gary Cooper and Jimmy Stewart developed as personalities, playing themselves role after role. At the same time, they were fine actors and fine technicians.

I've often been asked why the film industry hasn't generated more acting talent. The answer is simple: the men at the top do not care. They live on the basis of product being made today.

There is a sad but true saying in the industry: "Is it good?"

"No, but we'll have it Friday."

It would be very naïve for anyone to assume that the motion picture industry is carefully cultivating a new Laurence Olivier or a Richard Harris or a Marlon Brando. Talent is contracted on a six-, eight-, ten-, twelve-week schedule; picture finished, they say goodbye. In their view, it is just not practical to spend money to develop talent. They've been lucky.

Today many actors are getting formal drama training. Unfortunately, college drama often imposes the notion that the stage is *the* world of arts. Films and television are beneath the stage. The drama student is conditioned by the proscenium. As a result he is often frozen tight when he wants to grow and play to other than three hundred faculty friends. The collegiate mystic overtones of Shakespeare and Molière trap him when he's eye to eye with a lens.

Drama students should be taught that they can work successfully with fine film directors, film-makers and television directors as well as Broadway directors. If the actor has a good film director, there will be a psychological proscenium. The actor will be standing in No. 1 on the motion picture floor. In 1970 there is no such thing as a dramatic actor in the proscenium as opposed to video tape as opposed to film as opposed to performing in a room with four ladies and a fat man or three hundred faculty members. An actor has to be an actor in all medias in 1970. His training should reflect it.

Professionalism has its penalties and abrasions as well as its rewards. Milton Berle is an actor who likes to do everyone else's job, and does an awful lot of them better than most people. He is right 90 percent of the time when he wants someone to cut, lift or light.

The older engineers are appalled by this. Nobody likes to be told by someone who isn't supposed to know. Let them be appalled! It's easy to go to the bullfights and sit in the stands; it's murder to get into the arena. And Berle has been in the arena a long time. He knows what he has to do to protect himself and he knows how. He doesn't guess that a klieg light is burning him up. He knows it from experience. He's learned enough to say, "You're not going to play this in long shot. A head to toe, and I'm going to close my eyes. You got to be in tight for that."

The ones who hate the Berles are the ones who don't want to admit they are making the wrong shot, that the actor knows his craft. I respect Berle—all of the Berles. They have the guts to spit it out, and the experience to make it stick.

Whether you're in the director's chair, in administration or staff, or the utility man who brings the coffee, these precocious nine-year-old children will kill for you if you respect their humanity and their needs.

When Judith Anderson did *Cinderfella* for me, playing the nasty stepmother, she fell in love with a dress that I'd had made for her role. I think it was a $900 dress. I gave her the dress with a card, "To a lovely lady." Often you permit a player to buy his clothes. This was a gift.

Soon after, she went on the road to do *Medea* in sixty-five cities. For nine months of the tour she did television interviews in every city, always remembering to talk about *Cinderfella*. To buy that exposure would have cost about $600,000. I estimate she gave us an additional half million dollars at the box office.

I have never known a professional actor who did not respond to kind and fair treatment, plus a little spoon-feeding. Aside from being flies in amber, actors are very human.

6

THE MILLION-DOLLAR HUG

Joe Mankiewicz once said, "A good director is a man who creates an atmosphere for work." To me, that's what it's all about. You start out by giving actors a million-dollar hug. You don't use them and later on start hugging them.

Yet the first hug is not with the actor, it is with yourself. You can't care about other people and their problems until you care about yourself as an individual. By wanting to project your own best parts, you are beginning to create that Mankiewicz atmosphere.

This transference is at the core of dealing with actors on the human level. Warmth, affection and understanding flow from it, and a two-way street of hugging develops.

You may wind up hugging each other as sons-of-bitches in the worst kind of battle, but beneath it is honest care and concern for each other and the film.

You find out about actors by sitting with them on the set or over coffee in their dressing rooms. To learn about them, all you have to do is ask. Being actors, they'll tell you. Aside from the President of the United States, no one seems to have as many problems as actors. The director has to become a Beatrice Fairfax in addition to calling camera cuts.

Not too long ago I had a young actress, a newlywed, in a picture. I woke up one morning to realize I'd been spending a half hour a day in her dressing room yakking about everything but the film. I'd forgotten some shots; should have been thinking about some technical things. Yet I got a fine performance out of her. I'll never know how much the dressing-room discussions contributed to that performance but I think it did.

Funny thing, I've found that these complex flies in amber rarely admit to themselves that they are being spoon-fed, pacified and placated; that the director is actually subservient to them. They may know it, and hate it, but can't admit it.

So you start with flowers, hugging, kissing, telling them they're the greatest in the world. It's selfish, yet it's selfless. *They are fooling with your film.*

The director's cry:

"Do we love actors?"

"Yes, we love actors!"

"Will we kiss their asses?"

"Yes, we'll kiss their asses."

We'll do whatever has to be done to get the best possible picture into the cans.

As an actor, I know about spoon-feeding and getting an occasional break in the schedule. I know what it means to have time off.

When I'm directing any of the characters Jerry Lewis plays, I have to let the comedian run a little bit because I know him. When I lay out the schedule I see that they have me dealing with that comic Jerry every day. I yell, "Hold it a second. Let The Idiot rest one day, or let him play ball, or let him do what he has to do. He's nine years old."

I know what I can get out of him as a comedian. He is not a machine. He needs some playtime in order for me to get spontaneity from him. "Don't give him a call tomorrow. Let him sleep in."

So, we give Lewis the comedian a call for eleven o'clock, but send Lewis the director to the set at six-thirty.

Needless to say, to make a fine picture you must get the actors rooting for you, and spoon-feeding is but a part of that. Sometimes, in the most devious, lovely, lying ways, the director must let them know he is terrible and they are brilliant. And because of his inability to function, would they please try the same scene again? And while doing so, would they be so kind as not touch their hair?

There are times when you make believe that you aren't aware the actor simply doesn't know how to perform a particular bit of action. Instead of challenging him, you help him by admitting you don't know either. This can be like swallowing lye. But I've found it isn't profitable for the director to say, "Drop that ego." *He* has to drop it.

If the director is up-tight, he's wise to admit it. He doesn't necessarily have to be articulate—just, "Baby, I'm jumpy this morning. I've got a strong energy for this; I'm excited about it. If I don't excite you, tell me that and we'll go another route." Nine times out of ten, the actor will break his neck to help. But if you submerge that edginess, don't explain it, the actor dips into his bag of suspicion for an answer.

The day Judith Anderson walked on my set I had lockjaw. "Where do you want me to stand?" she asked.

"I don't care."

That was not as bad, I suppose, as the day I had Everett Sloane, rest his soul, standing one place and John Carradine to the side. The two of them were waiting for me to move them. I was dying, and it wasn't my first job as a director. I admitted I was dying, and I hope the crew wasn't watching when I asked them to sign my autograph book.

A new director is going to run into this problem. He has to tell the truth to his actors. "I'm impressed with you, Mr. Steiger, and I'm scared to death because this is my first movie. But I'm a good man and I know what I want and know what I can get. I love you, and think you're the greatest actor in the world . . . but you can't have my balls."

The response of any good professional actor will be surprising. He will admire your honesty and have respect for you before the camera turns. Be it Rod Steiger, or anyone else, he is also delighted to know you are frightened, too. He has a certain amount of fright on that first day. Unity and camaraderie develops.

This sort of thing works in front of the camera as well as behind. In that picture with Everett Sloane and John Carradine, I had a young actor who was new and consequently frightened and unsure. Peter Lorre, Phil Harris, Keenan Wynn and Ina Balin were also in the cast. That's enough experience to frighten anyone.

After one take I said to the young actor, "That's not what I want, but it's not your fault because I don't think I really communicated. It was my fault. Let me lay it on you again."

He blew it again, and I needed a jolt. I couldn't use the same approach. I didn't plan it but instinct turned me toward Sloane. I said, "Everett, this last time he was doing fine but you threw him. You forgot the pace I told you about. Keep it moving."

Sloane knew that he was perfect but answered, "Yeah, I see. I know. I was off. Okay."

Then the boy was fine. He'd heard the old pro made a

mistake. Everett, operating from intuition, didn't need to be asked to play straight man.

Samantha Eggar did a film entitled *The Collector*. Before the end of the first day Willy Wyler, the director, realized she was performing far below her ability. She was frightened. He called Kathleen Freeman, an old friend of his and mine. She's a fine character actress and I've used her in a number of films.

Kathleen worked with Samantha on a human level for about four days, telling her nothing more than: "There's no crime in being frightened. Your talent is not lessened by the fact that you're scared to death." Samantha's magnificent performance in *The Collector* is due, in large part, to Kathleen Freeman's help.

Some directors have wonderful tricks and devices for pulling performances. Norman Taurog is an expert. When he wanted to make me cry, he'd take me into a corner and ask me to think about what would happen if my little boy was hit by a truck.

The young, new film-maker does not necessarily have to start at the bottom. His first film can be with a top-rated, powerhouse actor or actress. Talent knows no age or particular experience level. He doesn't necessarily have to begin with three or four minor films before pitting himself against the heavyweights. He won't be signed to direct the top-rated actor unless there is a belief in his ability. He'll learn more from the heavyweight than from the actor who can't make it beyond fourth featured billing.

I've noticed one big fear on the part of young film-makers—they're afraid to spill their guts in front of an actor. They think the actor will take advantage if they open up. He may well take some advantage but he won't be the eventual winner. The chance must be taken.

Spilling out what's inside you, where you're at, is a gutsy thing to do, but to even contemplate going into films is gutsy. The young film-maker is deluding himself if he doesn't understand that the industry is precarious. At its worst, it grinds people into pulp. At its best, it is the most marvelous, exciting profession on earth.

Actors bring their set of tools—experience, information, attitudes, body and script. If they do not have the right attitude, or have an improper idea of the characterization, they need immediate help. The question of how much they should know about the total film always arises.

Obviously I cannot speak for all directors, but when I go into a film I let the actors know I'm about to give birth and that I want them to join me. I don't expect the actor to sympathize or necessarily agree with my view of the total film. I know he is more interested in his individual portrayal, but when he accepts his role he accepts the total film.

I try to give as much information as possible and usually have a full-scale reading of the major roles and a discussion before filming begins. A lot of bugs are nailed down and gotten out of the way. Throughout the filming I have meetings on the set or in the dressing rooms. Sometimes I have them before the daily start of shooting. The larger the star, the more willing he is to come early.

One problem I have with dramatic actors is keeping them straight to play against comedy. They tend to pick up the comic's tone and attitude. Then everyone is getting comic. There is nothing straight to play off.

With a film like *Death of a Salesman,* which was on Broadway two and a half years, it is a pretty good idea to have a long rehearsal before shooting. Perhaps four weeks. The story is locked and designed before the director touches it, and there is only one way to shoot it. Minimum shooting time is gained by maximum rehearsal time while filming a hit play.

Rehearsals can be filmed. I often do that to gain spontaneity. But it is tough to rehearse on film unless the actors are really up to the dialogue, the camera movement and all the technical aspects. Some footage may be wasted but sometimes there is a performance so spontaneous that it could never be directed. Once actors are aware the camera is grinding, the value often diminishes.

The main thing in rehearsals is not to kill the actor's spontaneity, deaden his material and his ability to rise above it. Most often, the very best rehearsal is the one just before the take.

But the director must always stage the scene. He can never let the actors stage it because he will not retain control over it. I had a director who asked, "How do you see this?"

I answered, "From an actor's standpoint. I see it's funny."

"No, how do you see it staged?"

I had to tell him, "I'm not the director. You want to see how I see it as a director you put on my funny clothes and I'll sit in your chair. Now, tell me to do something."

Judith Anderson, one of the great ladies of the stage and screen, does not budge without direction. She'll never walk out of position without being told to. She listens. No wonder she's acquired world stature.

Yet I don't believe you should tell actors, "Do it this exact way!"

The director should give the design, stage it, and then let them bring their individual contributions to it. As long as they do not steer away from it, he should assume the role of monitor.

There are many types of actors, but I think they can be broken down into those who are technical and those who act solely from within. The technical actor doesn't need any great warm-up in rehearsal. Trevor Howard is a male Loretta Young, geared up at any time. Marlon Brando is not. The rehearsal has to take both kinds into account.

Of all the information a director can bring to the set, the best information is the point of view of the performer. That doesn't make Richard Brooks, who has never acted, a lesser director. He is a great director, one of the best in the world, but he'll never understand petulance. He'll never really understand temperament or being made to feel like a two-dollar whore. Right or wrong, actors often feel this way.

The actors must know how the scene is being covered. If not, they may spit out everything in the master shot, which is the comprehensive coverage.

If you tell the girl that you are making a master of the boy and girl, followed by a single of the boy, a single of the girl, and a tight two, she'll save something for the snug stuff. She won't let the tears go in the master. She'll whine a lot in that one, which will be matchable, but then sob it out in the close shots.

I speak from personal experience. If I'm going to go facially, visually crazy I won't do it in a head-to-toe shot. Neither will I dance my best in a close-up. A professional actor's experience lets him know how to pace himself in the coverage of a scene if that coverage is explained to him.

I've heard that Fellini doesn't tell his actors very much about what's happening, and what will happen. Maybe that's right for him. Maybe his experience is such that he can move his camera, wing film, and get the results without great explanation. But it doesn't work for me, and I doubt that it works for most directors. I think the actors want to know.

Why does a director usually start with a master? My answer is that he wants to know where he is going. Without the master shot of the scene, the overall comprehensive, he has no guide to individual shots or other combinations. Total coverage of the scene evolves from the master shot.

Making films is locked into great technicality and there's always the question of how much the actor should know about the technical problems of coverage. Usually it burdens the actor to go beyond the instruction, "That's your mark." The complicated camera movement facing the director should be a matter between the director and the technicians.

The move becomes self-evident but should not be a factor in the actor's performance. The technicians should watch the cast rehearsal, and the cast should watch the technical rehearsal.

Some actors are very much aware of the technical complications of a difficult trucking shot, a shot where the camera is moved over a distance. These actors instinctively fall into a walk pattern, or turn pattern, after watching several technical rehearsals.

When I'm directing I literally mark a pattern for an actor's walk. I have him understand he is not a mental cripple, that he requires chalk marks in order to move; rather, the critical lenses being used require his assistance on an exact, methodical level. Then I tell him to forget the marks, go on to the importance of the scene, and how it is to be played. But just before rolling for a take, and after he is secure on the performance level, I remind him of the marks.

"Oh, those? Okay."

It works.

If a director needs coverage on only a few lines in a sequence, he's wise not to tell his actors, nor should he function as if that is the case. Actors are not motors to rev up and be cut at a time when they are peaking. They should go the route, the director absolutely knowing that he doesn't need all the material.

There is no way to draw a line between the technical things an actor should know and those that should not concern him. Generally the more he knows, the better his performance. Technicalities become a matter of instinctive "do-nots." Some actors do not even know when they are out of camera range. The first rule is, "If you see the lens, the lens sees you." Unless they are name actors or unless you have worked with them before, it is difficult to determine just how many technical tools are in any actor's bag. You find out the hard way.

The greatest asset any actor can bring to a set is his ability to listen. It is hoped he has more tools in his bag than listening power, but that is the first one he has to use. Without it, you can't do scenes. The head man in the director's chair is useless.

Almost always there is rivalry between actors. We return to the child syndrome. You attempt to keep it within reason by equal treatment. After you've done a scene three times and print a take, telling one actor he was marvelous, it's wise to also comfort the other actor. If he looks dissatisfied, you make another take, asking him to play it stronger, knowing full well you'll use the previous take. It has cost a minute and a half but you've sustained a relationship. I have made six or seven takes simply to satisfy an actor's ego.

I've also found it wise not to talk in front of actors except in generalities. If an actor is in trouble, I take him aside, perhaps into his dressing room. I may tell him a bald lie: "The trouble is the other actor. All I want you to do is help him be better." In his heart he knows he's at fault.

Naturally, some actors are weaker than others and have to be handled differently, often kept in the back a bit. This occurs film after film. Others, even very experienced players, have the jitters the first two or three days. I shot around John Carradine for three days until his nerves were settled.

Yet sometimes an actor gets so up-tight that he takes the control from the director. Each director has his own method of handling this, I suppose. Take five minutes! But never take five minutes because it's the actor's fault. I knock over a lamp. I am a champion at knocking over lamps. "Jesus, I didn't see that." It breaks the tension and you've got five minutes to set up and get going again.

As a comedian I have an advantage. When I'm straight, no one ever presumes I'm kidding, or being deceitful.

Often, when I have an up-tight actor, I say, "Turn around here, and just think for a second." A hand wave to a laborer on the set will get me a call. "Hey, Jerry, your wife is on the phone." I excuse myself and return ten minutes later to a calm actor.

But let's say you hire an actor and find that he is terrible. Hopefully, you can fire him. However, there are times when you don't have that luxury. If it isn't your show, if you're working for someone else, you may have to live with the bastard, even though he is endangering everyone else.

You have to be careful and diplomatic about it, let him think that he's in every shot, but in reality he is no longer in the picture. What do you do? Let's say a particular scene has two people in it. You shoot the master and get a couple of singles. You make his but do not get a single of hers. You play over him on her, so you keep him in the scene, but dub in another voice later. You get a single of her over him, and then a pop of him watching, as if he's listening. You play the scene on her almost entirely and he doesn't realize he's out of the film until he sees it in a theater. That's lousy, but you are protecting the total film.

Short of that, when these flies in amber need a verbal spanking, it has to be done with outraged dignity. I remember telling an actor: "Goddamn it, you have bent me four times now and I'm not going to take any more of your shit. Now, let's do it my way." He was a star and we did it my way.

I always deliver the first spanking in a far corner. If a second one is needed I make certain it is in the middle of the set where everyone hears it. Actors, like children, sometimes test to see how far they can go. If it goes too far, it infiltrates the rest of the cast and the crew. Suddenly control is lost. By and large, an actor wants the director to have firm and complete control.

It is not a matter of set discipline alone. Actors sometimes decide to change characterization, very subtly, for reasons only the actor and his God can know. For four weeks he's been playing a sympathetic character and suddenly one day he decides to add a little Bogart. Obviously, he has to be knocked down. He can play Bogart in his next film!

One way to keep actors in character is to invite them, if not order them, to see rushes each night. Directors who do not want their actors to see the dailies are basically insecure. He doesn't want to have an actor say, "Can't we do that scene again?" Any man who works in the creation of a film should be given the right to see what he does.

To a degree, the insight you get in directing yourself helps in directing other actors. At the same time, there is a contradiction because you don't really think in terms of directing yourself. You refer and must refer to that "other being." He is another entity. He is called The Idiot or The Kid. He is another person.

I assure you I have less trouble directing Jerry Lewis than the trouble we—the company, the studio, the producer—have when Jerry Lewis is directed by a stranger. He seems to come unglued because he tends to distrust that stranger.

I retain objectivity because The Idiot is another person. Dick Powell said that he could retain that director-actor objectivity. The same thing held true with Chaplin for years. I think that man with the baggy pants and floppy shoes and cane was another person to Chaplin.

If I get a director that I respect, a director who cares as much about the film as I do, it's a snap for both of us. But directing The Idiot myself is really more fun.

PRE-PRODUCTION CHORES

Between casting chores, writing or polishing the script, thinking about selecting the crew, listening to contract beefs and watching the budget rise, pondering location work, you're juggling set design, set decoration and wardrobe.

In some studios the art departments and other departments have too much influence and restrict the director in his choice of shots. In the last five years, with independents picking their own staff top to bottom and operating out of private offices instead of studio menageries, that influence has subsided. However, the effects of the system and the power of the studio art department and art directors will be felt for years. So you'd better know your racket as well as theirs.

Generally, the studio art departments do not want the director to invent unless he invents their way. Supposedly that attitude is based on saving dollars. Truthfully, it is more a matter of the art department's bureaucracy fighting against the director's individuality. What they do, time and time again, can be found on the second page of that courtroom scene in Ayn Rand's *Fountainhead*. It is a suppression grown out of years of system.

I think you must pick the art-department brains, use any good ideas, but battle every inch of the way to prevent the art director from steering the creation into the toilet to save a few dollars. Take their story-board, sketches of their ideas on how the scene can be played within the set, and use it as a departure point but not as a bible.

You know what you want to see, know what you want to photograph, know what you need to utilize the set, so in your mind you compose the construction. You don't need to be an architect or know quarter-inch scale. That is the nuts-and-bolts operation of the art director. You do have to have a firm idea of what you need for every scene in the film.

I build sets in miniature. I take cardboard and cut out rooms. This kitchen will work great with that dining room; this bedroom and that living room can work together. The cardboard sets tell me two can be revamped and redecorated for other uses at a savings in money.

The Ladies Man was a one-set film, shot entirely in a four-story, open-faced building which stretched across two Paramount sound stages. I'd always dreamed of a million-dollar set, and this one cost nine hundred thousand. It afforded me shots in and out of all the rooms, and to photograph it, I had a special boom extension built, possibly the largest ever constructed for a film.

To fully utilize this unusual set, and get the production values back from nine hundred thousand, I built a half-inch scale model of the entire set, then did all preparations with the model. Camera movements were blocked out; reverses, dolly shots, boom shots. I moved the model walls to detail the work. It proved to be a lifesaver.

It requires imagination more than a degree in architecture. I study issues of *Better Homes and Gardens* and other magazines to get ideas for sets. They can be offered as alternatives.

The same approach can be applied to set decoration. Every person involved in film-making has his own tastes and sometimes these personal preferences intrude on the story and on the director. Again, it is a matter of fighting to gain what is right for the film. If you have a hunting-lodge scene, a father and his son at Lake Arrowhead, you probably want throw rugs and a painting of Washington crossing the Delaware rather than a Cézanne and deep-pile carpets. That's a simple, obvious example, but you'd be surprised how often personal intrusions dictate sketches from art departments. Sometimes you wonder if you are both working on the same picture.

For male-wardrobe ideas I buy *Esquire*, for female-wardrobe ideas I buy *Vogue* and similar magazines. Time spent in dentists' waiting rooms can help young film-makers more than hours of lectures in classrooms. Perhaps it's impressive to walk around with *Cahier du Cinema* or the *Society of Motion Picture and Television Engineers'* journal under your arm, but you'll get more practical knowledge from everyday periodicals.

Location filming, to go or not to go, depends on the story and the budget. It's tough to photograph six hundred Indians attacking on Stage 2 at the Gold Medal Studios in the Bronx. There would be the problem of sky, horizon and the six hundred Indians, not to mention five hundred horses. Outside Phoenix with seven thousand acres of emptiness would seem more appropriate.

If you have to shoot two people on a BMT subway, the sound stage is the place to do it, not New York. You can build it cheaper and work easier on Stage 8. You can not only build the station but rent or build the train. The only reason to shoot it in New York would be to fill out four days of location work already scheduled in Manhattan. Of course, if the film is being made entirely in New York, there is no reason to go back to Hollywood for the one shot of the BMT.

Often, *local locations,* areas within driving distance of the studio, are used for a few days' exterior filming. *Distant locations,* of course, range from San Diego to Helsinki. The use of either depends solely on the story, the film-maker's desires, and money. Frequently it is less expensive to go on location, using existing buildings as sets, than to build them at the studio.

How the West Was Won could not have been made entirely in any studio or on any back lot. *Who's Afraid of Virginia Woolf?* didn't need to go around the corner. Some films have as much as 90 percent location work, 10 in the studio. Others have one percent location work, 99 on the lot.

Some studios and directors have spent bundles for film they could have just as easily shot on the back lots and in sound stages. Rue Pigalle can be made at 20th Century–Fox and look as good as Paris. But then the producer and director can't go to Paris at the expense of the picture, and neither can the studio executives.

Location filming does generally provide better atmosphere, better photography and, often, better working conditions. The director is out from under the department heads and studio execs. They aren't breathing in his ear lobe.

Currently few films are made in black-and-white for theatrical exhibition. Audiences worldwide want color. Any film that I produce will pick up another two hundred thousand in the Asian market simply because of color. I suppose black-and-whites will continue to be made now and then just for novelty.

I do not know how to show life in black-and-white. From birth to death, nosebleed to being hit by a blue Mercedes-Benz and buried in a green casket, life is in color. In one sense, there has never been a black-and-white picture. It comes out in shades of gray. The nearest I've ever been able to get to a true black-and-white is when I shot the black-and-white set in color for *The Ladies Man*.

Japan's Akira Kurosawa has said he does not like color, and up to 1968 had never made a film in color. Fellini doesn't like color. He has made the statement that films cannot be done in color as well as in black-and-white. Several European critics compared the use of color in *The Ladies Man* with Fellini's use of it in *Juliet of the Spirits*. Whatever that estimate means, I cannot see how any film-maker can deny the audience by staying with black-and-white. Life is color. (Documentaries are another story!)

Naturally, color becomes a taskmaster in the areas of wardrobe, set color and set decoration. In black-and-white you were primarily concerned about style, shape and surface; in color, it is shading and tone. What clashes, what doesn't? But even old rules of never putting polka dots with stripes are being broken. A film-maker is told, "You can't put green with blue." He does it anyway and it works. Then everyone else does it.

I have an inexpensive way of attempting to determine how colors will work. I buy different-colored handkerchiefs and put them together to see what jars my eye. It could turn out differently on the screen but that's the gamble. Often, the director's guess is just as good as the guess of the art director or cinematographer.

Some people in Hollywood agree with Fellini and still think that color is a distraction, that black-and-white achieves better dramatic values. It matters little what they think at present. The vast majority of films are being made in color and it won't change. Even so, I've never bought the theory that a red couch will take attention from the two people sitting on it. The audience will see the red couch and then go on to the drama exchange between the characters on the couch. If they aren't interested in what the people have to say, it isn't the fault of the color but of the script and director.

I have seen art directors design sets, select the colors, and finally, while they are being painted, yell, "Pour more white. It's too blue." You wind up with a dumb blue, a pastel. Fear! It's the hangover from Hollywood's black-and-white days, days when all the rugs were tan and all the walls light-green.

There are other rules. Murder mysteries should have somber colors! I think they need more color than comedies. By continually pushing it down, you wind up with washed-out color, sepias or halftones. Color is another part of the magic, the majesty of making films, and should be used that exact way.

Sometimes you have to gamble with color because it still

remains, largely, an unknown quality, dependent on many factors. You have the insurance of processing. When the dailies are returned, if they are hot, overdeveloped, or cold, underdeveloped, you can reprint, raising or lowering the color intensity. Processing can fix most color problems.

Next to the screenplay writer and the choice of lead actors, the most important assignment is the choice of the cameraman, the cinematographer. It is usually the director's choice, although the star may request a specific cinematographer. If he, or she, has enough power, that choice can be dictated. It does not happen too often. I'm the only director in Hollywood, at present, with a cinematographer under a fifty-two-week contract, although he only works about twenty of those weeks. He is available, knows how I work, what I want. I compose and he lights, and he's done some magnificent things. Every director should be able to control his picture, and every good director sits on his camera and composes his shots.

I'm not impressed by tales that Alfred Hitchcock doesn't feel the need for it. Norman Taurog prefers to let the cinematographer create his setups. He lays down ground rules for them and seems to get results—at least, in the films I've made with him. Yet I don't agree with his method.

In pictures I direct I do not allow any cinematographer to get behind the camera until after I position it, select the lens, set it for marks; frame high, low, left or right, and then lock it. After that, he can light.

No matter Hitchcock's or Taurog's method, I'm not alone in demanding camera control. Norman Jewison, Stanley Kubrick, Joe Mankiewicz and Billy Wilder are others who compose the scene shot for shot, move for move, and mark for mark.

I feel that the moment a director tells his cinematographer, "This is what I'd like to see," the director is no longer composing the shot. He abandons a creative responsibility.

Each director has his own way. I rehearse the actors; do a scene and watch it through the viewfinder, the director's most important mechanical tool, and mark the camera positions that I need. I then dry-run it with the crew, staging the actors in position and marking them. I start the scene, making the camera moves; check the frame and action, settle it, and then get out of the hair of the cinematographer. The stand-ins go to the positions and he lights it.

Of course, rehearsal before or after the camera setup depends on the scene and material. Rules are dictated only by the scene and material. I never rehearse a comedy sequence up to "full tilt." I get all the bodies moving and words said, and the comic does not step in until the take.

Neither are there any rules for camera placement other than space—a closet confines you and a prairie doesn't. The design of any camera setup or placement has to meet the incoming material and the outgoing. If you keep coverage of the scene in mind, your angle is as good as the cinematographer's.

The secret to operation around a camera can be held in one hand—a *viewfinder*. Without it, you can't stage, nor can you talk sense to the cinematographer. Without this tool, it is all speculation. With it, you can stage, plan design, and lay out well-organized homework. It is the director's primary mechanical tool, and the camera's ground glass is supplementary. The new director will find that a second-hand 35 mm viewfinder is worth more than a dozen textbooks.

Directors should not have to know lighting beyond the common sense of what their eyes tell them. The cinematographer, standing with his light meter, his own special mystery, generally knows when an actor is being "burned up." He also knows when the entire set is "too hot," or too dark. Ultimately you both find out at rushes.

It is difficult to set an absolute on the amount of time necessary to light. If you do an "A" picture, you don't talk to the cinematographer about his lighting time. You aren't doing yourself a favor if you interfere or try to rush him. If you've got a $110,000 budget, an A. C. Lyles production with Bruce Cabot, you tell the cinematographer, "We're doing sixty-four pages." He'll get the message because he's already using an Eveready from his armpit and shouting that he's lit.

There are many cinematographers who are tremendous creators in addition to being first-rate technicians. Haskell

Wexler gave Mike Nichols information during *Who's Afraid of Virginia Woolf?* that helped make *The Graduate* such a hit. With cinematographers like Wexler, who has since graduated himself into total film-making, you go a long way on faith.

Yet the director must know what's technically happening with the lights and camera. Mistakes in this area are often made because the cameraman and the director are not conferring enough. In *Funny Girl* you'll see a thousand diffused shots of Barbra Streisand as opposed to hard, sharp ones of Omar Sharif. They distract.

Certainly, you diffuse one side of the shot to make the girl pretty but you don't make the complementing cut of the man razor-sharp. Conference at camera can prevent it. So the cinematographer and the director had better be talking to each other, respecting each other's talents and contributions, and remembering who's the boss.

Another technical area that the director must stake out and claim for his own is the choice of lenses. To claim it, though, he has to know what they can do, and their limitations. His viewfinder and the ground-glass will indicate the coverage of a particular lens but they tell only half the facts. Things get tricky.

You have an actress coming from twenty feet upstage and don't want to lose the attitude of the man in his downstage position. What lens? If you follow focus on the lady, you lose the man! Obviously you select the widest possible lens and hold them both.

The only rule here is to put one on and try it. There is no arbitrary choice, no stroll with the cinematographer to say, "Twenty-eight? No, let's try a thirty." You know you need width, so you start with the thirty. Sit on the camera, take a look in the ground-glass, see the action, see the actors, everything is animating, and you are a hair snug. So you go to a 28.

The selection of lenses is determined by angles and subjects. A low angle on a woman often distorts. They are tough to shoot. The best way to photograph a woman is dead-on and close. Unless you are in a master and have eighteen people, nothing less than a 40 should be used on women. Cast a pretty girl, use a 35 on her, and she's apt to look like Ma Kettle. For reasons unknown, women distort easier than men.

Visual distortion, when not dealing with fantasy or trying to sell something other than the words of dialogue, usually invites visual confusion.

When a director with a good knowledge of his lens complement is setting a shot, he assists many members of the company. Sound, for instance. With the proper lens, he won't be photographing the dangling microphone. He also saves time, therefore money, and can retain the design of his scene.

Some new directors put impossible demands on lenses. It's lovely to have the action in the foreground, stay on the man's face while he is saying something with his eyes; soften on him, leave him without camera cutting, harden on the girl, bring her down, and then equally develop focus on both of them. Great! But some new directors strap on a six-inch lens and wonder why they can't get it. The actor walks for seven miles and never comes closer than the waist. Each lens has a particular function, and the only way to discover that function is to discover its limitations.

The industry got excited when Panavision, Cinemascope and Cinerama were unveiled. They were big-screen novel processes, and soon it was proved they were just novelty. Gimmicks! So, it is in Panavision. Often, it turns out to be just a *bigger* bad movie.

If I'm going to do a joke that isn't particularly funny, I don't want it that big. If the joke is funny, it will play just as well on a postage stamp. Unless *How the West Was Won* or *The Russians Are Coming, The Russians Are Coming* are in front of the camera, I'm old-fashioned enough not to believe in doing anything with long lenses. Even *Russians Are Coming*, an almost flawless film, was hurt in the intimate scenes because of the screen ratio.

To me, Cinerama is a vomit. I look at it and wonder why the hell anyone bothered. After fifteen minutes, there is no emphasis, no clear meaning—just size and gimmick. Occasionally a *2001: A Space Odyssey* will come along. But even in standard ratio, the normal 1.85, that would have been exciting.

Paramount brought Panavision out and I made one of

the first tests with it. For *The Ladies Man* I needed a New York test of actress Pat Stanley. I was about sixty feet away from her with a two-inch Panavision lens, holding a fairly good set. I wanted a choker, a close-up, and tried it in rehearsal.

Moving the camera with my hand, I was holding her in the ground-glass. If my assistant hadn't put his hand between Miss Stanley and the camera I would have hit her. Yet in the ground-glass I was a mile away—still too wide. I couldn't choke her! I said goodbye to Panavision, having learned from it. A three- or four-inch Panavision lens won't solve it. There is movement and drift problem, as well as size.

When these bright minds go to market with their new concepts and ratios, they seldom think about the director's problem in staging—moving the performers properly to camera. They think in terms of the Grand Canyon and say, Put the people in it.

So, a young director who has been working in television with that small screen finds himself shooting in Cinemascope. Wow, man! Then he also discovers he doesn't know what to do with the instrument. If he's on a roller coaster it works by itself. Other than that, and especially if he's dealing with people, he has technical problems the size of the Grand Canyon and he still won't be able to photograph the people properly.

I cheer for technical advances and received the first technical award given to a director. At the same time, I think gimmicks should be labeled gimmicks. The new director, to save himself and his picture, should be wary, at least, when he's given a Panavision, Cinemascope or Cinerama assignment.

When a double ratio can be utilized, when the vast area can be played in Panavision or Cinemascope, and then the ratio returned to a standard Academy or 1.85 for intimate scenes, a real breakthrough will have been achieved. It may happen.

When I was a kid I looked through that thing with eight glasses that turn and all do different stuff. Everybody in our block walked around all day looking through it. I put it down because it didn't turn me on at all. Neither do multipanel devices in films, or, for the most part, split images. A human's God-given optics do not split images.

There are times when split images are effective, but they remain gimmicks. If the story can be punctured with them, as Richard Fleischer did in *The Boston Strangler*, and Norman Jewison accomplished in *The Thomas Crown Affair*, their use is completely valid. Otherwise, optical gadgetry is an indication of a director who is trapped, or can't tell it any other way.

Retaining audience attention through the simpler creative method of proper camera movement and lenses is not only more effective but far cheaper than resorting to the optical department and a specialist in tricks. Designing a film specifically for optics provides half a crutch for the first six reels and a full one by the tenth. Suddenly the concept is in the hands of optical departments.

Each aspect, of course, requires different handling. In working with 1.33 aspect of television, what is normally comfortable in a waist shot for features is possibly not productive or effective for TV. It has to be done in a choker.

Probably the best teacher for projecting the performer is Jack Webb. He always utilizes the camera as he did in *Dragnet* because he knows the importance of magnification, as opposed to diminishing images.

When an actor is doing a take, the director should not only consider the animation of the artist but What's it going to look like on the screen? While watching the scene six feet away, the director has to be aware that the actor is being magnified a hundred times. He must think in terms of the breadth and size of his player's expression—how they will look when projected, magnified a hundred times.

I've made some pretty bad comedy simply because I wasn't really aware how broad the facial expression would be when projected. In my early days I had some directors who paid little attention to the overbearing comic face. Six or eight feet away it didn't look that broad.

In Webb's work for TV, whether for 17-inch- or 21-inch sets, he took great care with magnification—one actor or three. He got everything on the screen in proper relation.

Largely, it is a matter of camera moves and timing. If it is an eight-second move with the camera boom or crab dolly, it is an eight-second move simply because it feels right to the director. There is no absolute way to judge it other than checking the moviola or seeing the film projected. First, it must *feel right.*

There is a marked difference between camera movement and timing in shooting for television, as opposed to shooting for the big, big screen. It is governed by the ratios.

So we come to a little item called *inserts,* such as the face of a clock. Some directors want to shoot everything in their picture, including the mongoose's armpit. I depart at this point because inserts should be shot by SPD, the special photographic department, and delivered to the editor to be cut in. And shot on another sound stage to avoid holding up work.

If the audience must know it's ten to nine, SPD should shoot a watch while the director goes with more important or less important work.

To make the same point himself, the director might have to get a large clock, if it fits into the set, stage his actor, have him light a cigarette in front of it, or do something to call attention to ten to nine. He has to light the clock, light the actor. Insert photography on another sound stage, however, will give him the same story point and perhaps at less cost. (Conversely, I like to do my own inserts, just to be sure.)

8

THE CREW

Any good director gets a professional family when he starts a film. They immediately check him out to discover how much information he possesses. They also want to know if he has balls. They will challenge him the first day and every day until the wrap—unless he proves he knows what he's doing.

I create a film by myself; yet I know I have this hundred-member-crew family with me, functioning because they believe I know what I'm doing. If they begin to have doubts, they don't function properly, and a good film cannot be made. Pay is the reward for their work but has little bearing on their attitude.

They will sense the fright of the new director and certainly give him every opportunity to be frightened. Ordinarily they won't let him stay that way long if they believe he *does* know what he's doing. They need him to help kick their own fears and doubts. Sitting in that canvas chair, he is Papa, Mama, Brother, Friend and Confidant to the crew as well as the cast.

Many crew problems arise because of the twenty-five-year veteran who is still doing a minor job. He will always introduce himself: "I've been in the business twenty-five years." With those few words, the director is in trouble. The quarter-century vet is a critic and he'll be doing eight-hour critiques on the director's work. He is the guy who stands about thirty feet away, half in shadow, half in light, nodding, "Tsk, tsk, tsk." That means he thinks the director is getting into deep water. He thinks so because he doesn't know the next cut, or how that particular cut will be edited.

It is vital to top this man on the psychological level. I've found the only way is to know something about his craft. This doesn't mean you have to know the ABC of the gaffer's job or understand fully what a head electrician does and how he does it, but it means you should be aware of his operation and function. In any other business a little knowledge may be a necessary thing. In films a little knowledge of everyone's job is imperative.

The key people in the crew, the cinematographer, gaffer, camera operator, sound recorder, property master, aren't likely to give static. The ones auditioning you because they aren't too sure of their own jobs are your static. Often, they are permit people, not the regulars—people who come in on a permit to fill in. They can sap you. I seldom have them on my crews for more than a day.

Then there is the guy who is afraid of screwing up. He may be a good man but doesn't want his department head to turn on static. Word travels fast from the sound stages.

A case in point: you want to do a particular shot; your mouth is watering to do it, and you want to use a crab dolly, a small mobile camera platform operating on a smooth floor or tracks. You want to dolly through a doorway, carry the people through it and into a room.

Peering at the doorway the key grip stands back and frowns, "The dolly is thirty-six inches wide and won't go through that door." Often the director will buy that excuse, revamp his thinking and make a cut instead of a continuous shot. The key grip has been around long enough to know that there are a number of ways to make the shot. He prefers the easiest. The doorway is thirty-seven inches wide, and he doesn't want to sweat taking that dolly through with a half-inch clearance on each side. His chances of screwing up are fair.

If the director knows the width of the crab, and the key grip is aware he knows it, the question of the difficulty of the shot may arise but it won't be dead before it's tried.

It doesn't hurt to keep a tape measure in your bag but it's disaster to walk over and measure the crab and the doorway in front of the crew. Further, if you come on too strong, they'll change the width of the doorway during the lunch break. They'll make it thirty-six inches.

Then there is the dingaling who thinks he must constantly call attention to his ability, speed and skill. There is one on every crew. He also has been around a quarter century.

I had a property man who was this type and I remember a thing with a pack of cigarettes. They were on a table in the scene and didn't belong there. Sixty people were running around. Make-up men were dabbing the actor and actress; the cameraman was making a last-second reading on his light; boom man was shifting the mike two inches. I'm waiting for it all to come together. Then my first assistant calls out, "Jerry, we're ready."

LEWIS: "Okay, clear them out."

Everyone not in the scene scurries out.

"You set, honey?"

"Yes."

"Ready, Wally? Carl?"

"Right."

"Yup!"

"Okay, here we go."

I get this far, about to say, "Roll," and this prop man sprints in to grab the cigarettes. Running off the set, he pants, "I got them out." Then the actor or actress thinks, He sure works.

LEWIS: "You couldn't have taken the cigarettes when everyone was busy with make-up?"

HE'S STUNNED: "Twenty-five years I've been doing this!"

There's no way to argue with him. He's a sweet soul, usually, and won't give you a lot of trouble. But he's there, and knowing how he operates will make the director's life simpler.

Now one of the key members of the crew, often the sound mixer or boom man, the guy that dangles the microphone, comes down: "I'd like it again." He has not seen that the camera hit the marks, that the performances were superb. *He* wants it again. If the director doesn't know the sound bag, he must make the shot again. He can't take the chance of not making it. If he does know the sound or boom man's bag, he asks, "Why?"

"Technical problem!"

"Well, spit it out. What is it? Do you have a broken cable? Didn't you get sound at all? Why didn't you stop me in the scene if you weren't getting sound?"

Likely it will be a very valid technical problem. But the boom man may say he didn't flip the mike, rotate it, over the girl's line. Then it's no problem because the scene worked beautifully in every other aspect, and the director can get the line in the girl's close-up.

Sound? What good's your picture without it? So you get the best possible sound man that you can afford. I sit with mine before a scene, particularly if it's complicated, and tell him what sound I want and what I don't want. I have one standing rule: Do not call for additional takes until you find out exactly what I need. Often the sound man requests another because of exterior noise, noise on the stage or a flubbed line. The latter I can hear as well.

But it may well be that I'm only going to use the front section of the scene, before the noise or flubbed line. I don't need another take.

On location the sound mixer is likely to say, "It isn't audible. I hear a lot of *shhhhh*."

"So we've got a lot of wind out here. As long as you can hear the words and they're clear, so we have *shhhhh* in it."

The mixer doesn't want the *shhhhh* because the head of *his* department will think he doesn't know his job; he hasn't used a wind-screen to block it out.

I think the wise director doesn't do anything on location that will necessitate looping, or duplicating the dialogue when the actor returns to the studio. All looping is done in a small room with three cable stands, a Sunkist orange crate and some dirt and rocks. The sound-effects men use the room to get footsteps or break glass when the actors aren't looping. It always sounds hollow.

If they photograph Michael Redgrave exterior at Orly Airport and then loop him later in the small room, there is no air, no wind. He sounds like he is talking in an empty space.

Make-up wants it again because the actor perspired. But make-up has to be pinned down beyond the generality of wanting another take. Perhaps that oozing sweat, a make-up man's nightmare, is just what you need for the scene.

To him, thinking only about his department head's recoil at rushes the next morning, it is a disaster.

Basically I think the director must rely on his own vision in competing with the twenty-five veterans. His eye will tell him when an actress has too much make-up, when the actor looks greasy. The director will never have the practical knowledge to add more freckles or put a dimple in. He doesn't need it. He does have to express his own tastes with make-up or anything else. In most areas, his gut judgment is absolutely as sound as the technicians'.

The camera operator is a highly important member of this team. He has to be skilled more than creative, although the latter helps. As much as the actors, he has to be a good listener. I had a camera operator who had a trigger finger. He thought he knew the scene and threw the switch before I could call a cut. He didn't last the day.

Another camera operator didn't finish his day down in Miami when I was doing *The Bellboy*. I was filming a Douglas plane, the first DC-8 delivered to National Airlines, and had it for an hour. Four cameras were covering and I was watching the action when I suddenly realized one of the cameramen was standing back, ogling like a tourist. He thought he had enough footage and hit his switch.

"I thought I had enough. Didn't you just want the takeoff?"

I yelled to my assistant, "Get him out of here. I'll kill him." Oh, Jesus, just the takeoff, when we only had an hour. As it turned out, I had enough from the other three cameras. But there was a possibility of disaster.

I used to think "Whenever you're ready, C.B." was a big joke. Since I began directing I don't laugh even a little bit at it. A light can go out, an actor can have a coronary, a jaguar can attack an electrician, but until the director calls "Cut," that camera has to roll. The instructions I give my operator are simple: "If the jaguar is eating your arm, use the other one." No one but the director can stop a scene.

There are times when the tail end of a scene can save blood on the cutting-room floor. A pretty good man taught me to always take a long swallow, spit silently, say, "Jesus Christ and where are the Jews?" and then, then only, call out, "Cut!" Let the actor die, let the bed burn up, but don't cut the camera the split second at scene's end.

I have bled on the cutting-room floor because I was cocksure I knew what I wanted, knew how I was going to use it, and had yelled, "Cut!" Once, I would have paid a hundred thousand dollars for three frames of film. Not having them ruined the scene, and the material in the sequence cost that much. Without those three frames, there was no delivery in the scene. Therefore, no scene!

Some directors take a pretty bleak view of all crews. I will quote one: "For the most part, crews walk on the lot at seven o'clock in the morning vowing that you'll never make the movie." I don't happen to share this opinion but there will be enemies in the trench with you. Most times they do not really mean to be enemies, but they are so involved in their own jobs that they don't relate them to the total.

It sounds great at the Academy Awards to hear a director walk up and say, "I couldn't have done it without my gaffer, thirteen electricians, the camera loader, utility man and the gate cop . . ." It sounds like everyone has knocked his brains out to help the director win his Oscar. In that pure sense, it was so much bullshit.

It may sound hard, cruel and cynical, but the crew members are knocking themselves out to help themselves. It isn't a good idea to go around proclaiming that philosophy, but it remains a fact and that's the way it should be. If they are a good crew, they have pride in their work and they want to work the next show.

Team effort, out of selfless pure love for the director, is a state of mind, and the director must acknowledge it but at the same time not be cynical about it.

At the end of the day there is only one guy who will have his throat cut for bad product grinding through the camera. He is the director. If for one reason or another the director is replaced, the crew will go on functioning on that film or go to another show. If the crew is fired they'll have another job very soon. The director may not.

I strive for a light tone on my sets. Have some fun. Relax everybody. A good crew that likes you will take on your tonality, attitudes and energy. If you are up, they're up. If you're down, they'll go down. So I try to make happy between takes.

If I'm in a black mood, I go *behind the set* on the way to the camera setup and try to shake the mood. If I can't get the rhythm of a scene, I'll call a break rather than fight a losing battle and lose the crew. I've even called for a lunch break at nine-thirty in the morning rather than muck up four hours.

Because of the loose, fun atmosphere on my sets, I usually have to clamp down at least twice during every picture. The atmosphere tends to breed advantage-taking. The crew is dealing with a double image—the man who is sitting in the director's chair, and the silly nut who is taking pratfalls. The images become confused.

I remember one of my clamp-down speeches: "Now, hear this, the next son-of-a-bitch that doesn't do as he is told will be taken bodily off the set. I'll see to it that he never gets a job again. Shut up and conduct yourself like professionals." A nice pause. "Now that you're through testing me, we'll get back to the fun of making pictures."

They walked like pussycats for four weeks, and then needed it again.

In dealing with the crew, there is a certain amount of winging and faking in the director's bag. There have been areas in which I've professed solid knowledge, or even expertise, and didn't know what the hell I was really talking about. Once I dropped "Well, I was a set designer in 1947." *He what?*

That game must be played with care. Obviously it's much better if you do know. I've found that most crew members will take the one piece of knowledge you know about their craft and bend your ear all day. They're anxious to reveal their full bag. They acquire a feeling of importance and that's half the battle of the relationship.

At first, the range of necessary acquaintance if not knowledge is staggering—sound, opticals, processing, effects, music, music scoring, dubbing, editing, wardrobe, make-up, casting, colors, sets and design. Yet there are no particular mysteries about any one technical area, and none requires a doctorate to understand the working knowledge.

The old-timers will hate the fact that you are twenty-four and hope that lightning strikes you. But if you know something they know, and beyond that, show respect for what they know, they hope you'll live to be a hundred. Pick their brains. Make their contributions appear of little worth and they'll sabotage you.

When it comes time to select crew and staff the wise director surrounds himself with those who know as much if not more, totally, than he does. Ego makes that hard to swallow and it's the kind of thing you never admit, even to yourself. But you'll make a better picture. Otherwise, the director can possibly find himself as weak as the weakest member of his crew.

The goal is to have a one-man project made with one hundred and two pairs of hands.

9

HOMEWORK

Homework, so far as I'm concerned, applies to preparation of the next day's material. However, it begins long before any camera is rolled. In one respect, it begins the day the story is bought, or the day the idea jells. All of the prior knowledge of the film goes into the homework for any specific day's shooting.

Again, each director has his own methods, but mine is to know the script to the point where I can recite it. I also mark my script an average of nine times over a period of about nine weeks of preparation. After these master markings I begin blocking scenes according to the film's schedule. I usually do not plan the essentials in terms of camera positions, movements and staging beyond the next day's work.

I draw every move of the camera on paper, visually preparing it for what I have already shot, and mentally preparing it for incoming material. It takes about two hours each night, and is based, generally, on the prospect of shooting four pages of script per day.

As an example, on November 10 I'm scheduled to shoot a love scene in the interior of a bungalow. November 9 I go home, study the scene as if I've never read it before (and perhaps I've written it), plot every move of the camera, every angle. Then I decide how I want to see the scene played on the screen, what I must punctuate, and most important, how it will fit into the film as a whole.

Prior to this night I have designed all the sets with angles and lenses in mind. I know I am working with a set twenty feet right to left, forty deep. I know I am not going to use an establishing shot with anything more than a two-inch lens at ten feet. I don't need more than that to indicate it is a bungalow. I decide, this night, that I won't move in the shot. I may cut to a snug shot of the girl, using a three-inch lens; then include her over him. I'll need a three-inch lens, a two-inch, and a forty. Of course, I can augment if needed. But as of the moment, this complement of lenses looks good. I list them according to the shot.

Aside from knowing what you're doing on the set the next day, the great value of proper homework is saving footage. That emulsion costs a bundle. Most wasted footage comes from uncertainty in shooting.

Of course, there is always George Stevens who will do inserts of a caterpillar's leg to cover dialogue of a lady screaming, "I like incest." Then there's the fellow walking down the street to clean up behind the elephants. "Well, pick up a cut of him, too." George shot nine hundred thousand or a million one hundred thousand feet on *A Place in the Sun.* I saw him in the commissary one day and asked, "How friggin' long can you drown Shelley Winters?"

The big danger of overcoverage is that you are trapped with cans of film and it becomes optically impossible, as well as mentally impossible, to fathom what the hell you've got. Pace goes out the window. You put in two and a half minutes of film for a minute-and-a-half scene. Simply because you've got it. That minute of stretch blows the pace.

However, the homework should remain flexible. After it is prepared, it should act as a guide and not a concrete set of shooting rules. The creative mind must stay unlocked because oftentimes many wonderful things will occur on the set. An actress may bring in a bit of business; an actor may deliver something completely unplanned. Homework has to be adjusted, or even completely abandoned, if the scene is not working. Occasionally the director gets so close to a scene that he misses the point it is making.

Many mornings my film editor strolls over to the stage to peek at the night's homework. It is dated and marked by the scene number. He likes to check for planning purposes in the cutting room. Often he looks at the prepared home-work and then the activity on the set: "Jesus Christ, what are you shooting?"

When it happens, the new setup is invariably better, but the solid homework at night has prepared the way for it. Spontaneity arises from preparation, in one form or an-other, but no professional film-maker depends on spur-of-the-moment to reach his end title. As a rough estimate, about 70 percent of what I shoot is prepared in homework. The balance is spontaneous, lightning striking on the stage, but is based on the other sweat.

Decisions constantly arise out of homework. If you have a four-page, three-and-a-half-minute scene, you may de-cide against shooting it in master. With a scene that long, you may not even have the luxury of shooting it in a mas-ter. Of course, there are also occasions when the master is worthless. No matter what, it is certainly insurance in the cutting room.

For TV, with a day and a half to shoot sixty-eight pages, you may well panic: "Shoot everything in masters." Sad day, because you'll panic in the cutting room. Yet televi-sion does not have the luxury of the feature stages and I'm amazed at some of the marvelous film turned out for the tube. I'll never understand how they do it, how they plan. They are geared for it, or else so technically oriented and grooved that they do not care. By and large, cutters are the heroes in that business. The director is off to another show when he wraps. The editors put it together.° (*I* put *mine* together with a great editor, Budd Small)

Very few films are made in complete continuity, starting with Scene 1 and progressing page by page through to the end. Not many films have a budget that can carry all the players for the full shooting schedule. If so, it's a wasteful budget. Money is tossed to the winds if an actor is hired at ten thousand a week for a ten-week picture and only works three weeks. Logically, he will be hired at ten a week for the weeks needed.

But it goes beyond the actor. If extras are used in the opening sequence, and the same faces are needed for the closing sequence, they must be hired for the full schedule unless the director goes out of continuity. A lot of money is wasted. He cannot gamble that he will have the same faces in two scenes ten weeks apart.

Set construction is also involved. If he shoots the opening sequence on Stage 16 and plans to come back to it nine weeks later, the set must remain standing. Stage rental is paid. Striking it, and rebuilding it eight weeks later, is insanity, too. Both the opening and closing sequences, if they are related, should be shot in the same time period and out of continuity.

° Since this book started I directed "In Dreams They Run" on *The Bold Ones*—N.B.C.—TV

For individual scenes, every shot in Mary's bedroom should go before the cameras day after day until finished although they will appear in four different parts of the film. Continuity is usually an ill-advised luxury and its only affirmative value is maintaining pace, attitude and tone value.

Out-of-continuity homework again must then deal in sequences of threes: what has been shot two weeks ago, what will be shot tomorrow, what must be shot two weeks hence. The script breakdown—done in pre-production by the assistant director with an eye to actor costs and availabilities, set construction, availability of exterior locales and a few unknown factors, such as weather—is a guide to the work schedule.

But the color, look, tempo and texture of tomorrow's work can only be found by looking at film that might have been shot two weeks ago, two months ago. A portable projection booth on the set provides a reminder to both the director and the cast. No director or actor can trust his memory by the end of the week. The director should attempt to develop a retentive memory, almost a photographic memory, but he is foolish to trust it when doing a scene that ties in directly with, or is a continuation of, a previously filmed scene.

Aside from its application to homework, a retentive memory saves trauma in the screening rooms. On the sound stage the director tells the operator, "Frame hard left. Hold on that pillar. Don't go beyond because I want to leave air." He had better remember what he told the operator. At the dailies when he sees air on that left side and screams, the operator will be happy to remind him about the pillar. G'wald!

On the sound stage he tells the script girl, "Print Take Four; hold Five." It becomes a pencil mark on her script. It had better become a mark in his brain, too. If the humanities are bad, she just may cross him and print Take 3, then swear that's what he said. Who can prove it? She has the mark.

I've developed the trick of associating shots and the numbers that relate to them. After a shot I'll take a quick look around and associate something with the take number. If it's a sweep, I'll do a 180 degrees, see what's there and mentally tag it with the print number.

When filming I'm never more than several feet from my script and homework. A property man has the job of keeping that bound leather book in sight. I refer to it often except on those days when the night juices have changed and I'm going the spontaneous route. I suppose each director is different. George Cukor comes on the stage carrying three pages of script, his day's work. He doesn't bother to bring the whole script. Every man for himself!

I've been asked if I'd do a film differently. Plan it differently? Shoot it differently? It's like the newsman who asks, "If you could live your life all over again, would you do . . . ?"

THE SHOOTING SCRIPT—working with camera angles on the set
(see following page)

CAMERAS—
from the
large
to the
small

THE OPEN SET—all my sets, whether on location or in the studio, are
open to the people

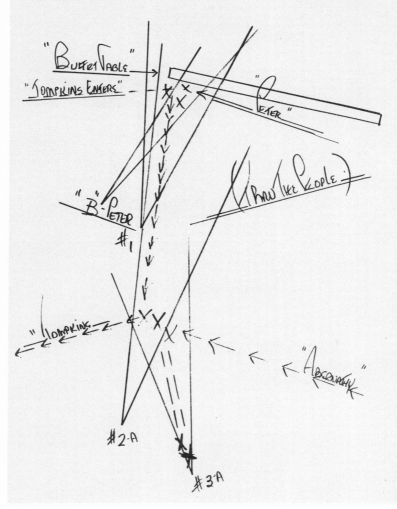

Two facing pages from shooting script from *One More Time*

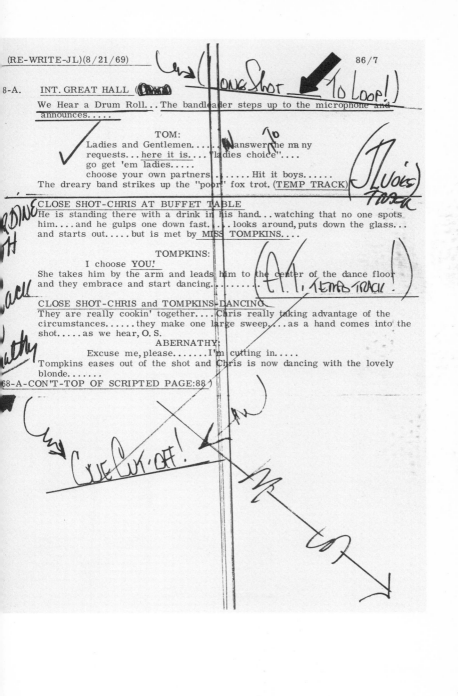

8-A.   INT. GREAT HALL

We Hear a Drum Roll...The bandleader steps up to the microphone and announces.....

> TOM:
> Ladies and Gentlemen.....To answer the many
> requests...here it is...."ladies choice"....
> go get 'em ladies.....
> choose your own partners.......Hit it boys......
> The dreary band strikes up the "poor" fox trot. (TEMP TRACK)

CLOSE SHOT-CHRIS AT BUFFET TABLE
He is standing there with a drink in his hand...watching that no one spots him....and he gulps one down fast....looks around, puts down the glass... and starts out.....but is met by MISS TOMPKINS....

> TOMPKINS:
> I choose YOU!
> She takes him by the arm and leads him to the center of the dance floor and they embrace and start dancing........

CLOSE SHOT-CHRIS and TOMPKINS-DANCING
They are really cookin' together....Chris really taking advantage of the circumstances......they make one large sweep.....as a hand comes into the shot.....as we hear, O.S.

> ABERNATHY:
> Excuse me, please.......I'm cutting in.....
> Tompkins eases out of the shot and Chris is now dancing with the lovely blonde.......

8-A-CON'T-TOP OF SCRIPTED PAGE:88

THROUGH THE LENS—viewing a set as the camera really sees it

MIXING—adding sound to the picture is often
as crucial as editing the film itself

SPONTANEITY—
some of the funniest
bits are often not
in the script

FRAMING—
setting up a shot

Photo by Rolland Lane. Courtesy of Universal City Studios, Inc.

I answer, "Can you arrange it?"

"No."

"Well, don't waste my time. I have things to think about that are possibilities, not goddamn fantasies." I'm thinking about the project that begins next Tuesday.

Once a film is in the can, it is history, good or bad. The design and homework for tonight and tomorrow are enough to handle.

10

FILMING IT!

Most directors use the master shot, the overall shot of the scene, to cover all of the action. They often find themselves in trouble if their pacing is too tight. If the master is loose, they retain control of it and have a chance in the editing rooms. This "looseness" is not a matter of players' timing with each other. Rather, it is the structure of the entire scene. A restricted master restricts the individual pieces that will be shot. Snugging and tightening can be done on the moviola.

Sometimes you'll see a film where the tempo is much too fast. In making *One, Two, Three*, Billy Wilder played it tight to the belly. Scene for scene it was flying. It was butt splice to butt splice, scene for scene—taking off, moving. Funny and good. But if he wanted to back off, slow it down, there was no way to go.

Camera cutting, editing in the camera instead of on the moviola, is dangerous enough, but improper pacing of a scene can be disaster. The director has to stand back and helplessly watch it fly by.

There are advantages to multiple cameras and also tremendous disadvantages. I did a multiple setup, an A camera and a B camera, on a sequence in *Three on a Couch*, covering it from two angles simultaneously. It was action with a hand, and a joke, coming down to the frame. It should have been a snap to cut since the footage was identical, except for the angles. In the cutting room I still found myself missing material needed to make the cut work.

I put the two picture tracks on a double moviola, and finally had to throw one of the six frames out of synchronization to make the two pieces match, but it wasn't perfect. So, I reshot the sequence after blowing ten days.

Multiple-camera use works beautifully head-on, for instance. Holding two people on a hundred-foot walk in a waist shot, and also in a head-to-toe, moving with them, can be done with double cameras without too much concern. It should cut perfectly. Separate the cameras too far apart and nightmares can develop.

In starting a sequence, after the actors are all burped and set in their places, the master should not be confining.

Juices may cook that are completely contradictory to the master as planned. Good directors will dump it as quickly as they will use it.

Sometimes the scene will cook in the singles, the two shots, the reactions and by-play. After it is completely finished, it can be re-staged in a master shot simply for safety in the cutting room.

When a setup is being planned, I think the best approach is to get the actors in position, play the scene and give them the marks, letting the cinematographer and crew see the action. Then position the camera! At times I've positioned the camera first and worked the actors toward it.

I doubt any other industry, or art form, has as many breakable rules. My camera setup is right; the next director's is wrong. Or we're both right and wrong. What matters is the material and what has to be shown. There are no ground rules: no rules to say you must pan if a man walks around a table; no rules to say the camera has to move in any direction. You may pan and then throw half the pan away and cut to a cat. It is, absolutely, the director's choice.

So, you make your setup, and I'll make mine. I usually go from the master to a medium to a close in cuts. Or I make a camera move from the master to the closer position. Any given day I'll do it differently, and my difference will be just as correct as the next director's.

Some film-makers believe that you should never have an

actor look directly into the camera. They maintain it makes the audience uneasy, and interrupts the screen story. I think it is nonsense, and usually have my actors, in a single, look direct into the camera at least once in a film if a point is to be served.

There is always the question of how the director should block out a scene: why people are placed in one spot rather than another. The only answer, likely, is a question: Why are they there? Another: What are they discussing? So it depends on the story and particularly on the needed effect.

Sometimes the director will want a static look to his scene. For an interior of *The Patsy*, I tried to achieve that effect by simply allowing "bodies to fall." The sequence was not designed around any of the characters, and I hoped it would be awkward, unsure, graceless. It failed miserably.

Not staging it—just letting the actors go through it—did not work. My actors altered it. They were substantial people and would chew each other alive if given the freedom. One of them was the late Peter Lorre, a scene thief beyond compare. He'd give a little pop at the lens, stroll this way, change his mind, go back. The other people around him weren't about to let him get away with it. So my static scene became something else and I altered tactics.

Except in rare cases, the scene must be fully blocked out—actors moving or holding on a specific line. They must be importantly placed. The director deals in exposition. He must spell out who they are, and what they are.

I saw the movie *The Odd Couple* and felt it cried for things to happen to the audience. It was not a matter of playing a two-shot instead of a master, but the overall designs of certain scenes. I doubt I would have noticed except that the director annoyed me by practically saying, "Hey, look at this!"

Walter Matthau is at the card table with three other guys when Jack Lemmon enters to say, "Helen left me!" Then sixty-five seconds of a minute-forty-second scene was played in the master with one guy picking his nose, another shuffling cards, and the third munching potato chips. I still cannot say what Lemmon was telling Matthau. It was the moment to establish a nine-reel rapport between the two characters but it was blown with card shuffling and potato-chip crackles.

I suppose it was being precious to stay in the master, but the whole design of the scene collapsed because of failure to get out of it and into singles and deuces of Lemmon and Matthau. I ended up not knowing who they were and what they were. Sitting in the theater, I was audience and not a film professional.

Straight cuts, those breathless snips of the avant garde, are sometimes discussed as if Antonioni invented them. They were around when automobiles had wooden spokes. "Straight-cut to . . ." feels and sounds easy, but it takes very special material to straight-cut to anything. All films are not quite Antonioni, and the young film-maker may suddenly become terribly young if he straight-cuts all his talents on the machine. Next time he cocks around with paper and camera, better he should also include *dissolve*, *fade in* and *fade out* in his vocabulary. Along with *establish*, *punctuate* and *resolve*.

It takes very special material and very strong focal points to straight-cut a film. Cary Grant has to grit his teeth if you're straight-cutting because that grit is an automatic dissolve; when John Wayne wipes his nose on his sleeve, it's an automatic flip and you're somewhere else.

You can straight-cut only when you have solidity in the center of the screen. Otherwise, the audience is asking, "Where are we now? I don't understand." Although shooting in straight cuts feels episodic, go out anywhere in the film, come in anywhere, truth dawns in the cutting room. It can't be done.

The only reason for various cuts of any scene is to avoid stagnancy on the screen. Yet, making them can be a time-consuming trap. There is a tendency to overshoot for cuts and a danger of having a "cutty" film as the result. Economy and breakdown of the script offer the guidelines of how many cuts are needed for a specific scene. Many times they do not require a new camera setup. As an example, for each of four different cuts the camera can be moved slightly, put to four different marks without breaking the setup. With creative angles, the results won't be static.

Young film-makers are sometimes trapped by a fear of

undercoverage and consequently shoot everything and anything. For example: a mother has to meet her young son downtown. The inexperienced director might take her down a stairway, put her on a phone, have her call a cab; get in the cab, ride away, stop the cab, pay the driver, have the cab pull away, and nine hundred feet later she's on a downtown corner saying, "Son, darling." It should be a line of dialogue, "I have to meet my son," and then a cut to the meeting. Eight hundred and seventy-five feet saved!

There seems to be a fear of simplicity in our current intellectual concepts of film-making. Unless it is complicated, says the avant-garde clan, it is not terribly valid. Jesus! A lot of young film-makers are finding that complication is not the answer to a good film. They are discovering it is no crime to place a Mitchell camera on sticks and have the actors work toward it. Nostril shots are no more avant-guarde than long shots. Simplicity makes better film: master, medium, choker. At least, men like Chaplin and David Lean think it does.

Actors or actresses have died in the middle of production or have become seriously ill. Skilled directors have finished the picture without the audience being too aware that one of the stars is missing. Doubles, look-alikes, in long shots, and clever work in the editing rooms have saved films in this type of trouble. It requires great ingenuity—shooting doubles from the shoulder down, or softly diffusing the foreground of the double—but it can be done.

There is still another misconception in cut coverage, one of those rules to be broken: it says that the director make a single shot of the male if he has made a single of the female. Each man to himself, but I prefer to do a single of the female and relate her to the male with an over-on, *over her on him,* at the same time keeping a single of her. With two singles there is no direct tie between the characters. If it is a long scene, you wind up with a single of her, single of him, back and forth. Over-on shots keep them together.

It's also a fallacy, I think, that an over-the-shoulder shot needs to be complemented by another over-the-shoulder shot. That's 1910.

As long as it works, is smooth, and doesn't confuse the audience, *any cut* can be made, no matter how controversial. Often a director will defend a cut, claiming he did it deliberately; invent a dozen reasons. Usually he has made a mistake and is attempting to gloss it.

Charlie Chaplin was the first great total film-maker, but in the last thirty seconds of *Modern Times,* one of his finest efforts, he made a direct reverse. It stopped the audience cold out of confusion. I have no knowledge why he did it, but assume it was simply a mistake.

A direct reverse, going from a man-and-woman camera right to the man-and-woman camera left, altering their positions in a direct cut, cannot work on the screen unless the picture is an Andy Warhol reject. It not only screams out confusion but screams out "cut." The secret is to move the film without the audience ever being consciously aware that a cut, any cut, has been made.

Too many beginning directors play with their cameras, moving them to let the audience know the camera is moving. They should have their hands broken, should have the cameras dumped on them. Again, it is that kid's shout, "Hey, lookit me!" Children and toys.

Yet I suppose every director dreams of making a 360-degree shot, that breath-taking camera pan all the way around the set. For the record, film buffs claim there are only seven or eight that have ever been used in the entire history of cinema. I made one. No one ever saw it except my cutter and myself because I threw it out.

It was beautiful. No one could tell who was in it, or what the dialogue was about, but it was a helluva shot. The scene was with Everett Sloan, Phil Harris, Keenan Wynn, Ina Balin, Peter Lorre and John Carradine. It took four and a half hours to do it. Until I saw it on the screen, I thought I was one of the greatest directors in America. Then I realized they all looked like Hubert Humphrey and it didn't fit in my film! I re-shot it in an hour and a half the right way. It killed me. My ego had run away, and there was no justifiable reason for the 360 except indulgence.

Chaplin seldom, if ever, indulged his whims with a camera. Every setup that he had in *Modern Times* was the center of the focal point. The only time he would be off center would be for delivery, never for composition.

For example, when we see the ambulance outside the

department store with a title card, "An accident occurred in the department store," he has opened on the ambulance dead center of the frame. The crowds are camera left and right, equal. A man is being carried out, and he pans left a hair to let Paulette Goddard say, "What's going on here?" But the action remained dead center.

Chaplin never painted pictures but he moved the camera considerably, always with a reason. He moved with the action, brought the action to the camera, and then continued to move it. Yet the audience is never aware of camera, only of the people and the action.

Often the beginning director will move his camera to cover up trivial exposition, busy it up to give it strength. It always backfires. Trivia should remain; shoot dull crap dull. Inventiveness and ingenuity should be applied to the important scenes. Overshoot importance, not junk!

Some collegians prefer films that are ad-libbed, winged all over the place. Fine, if it works! Winging rarely does work. It takes an expert to wing effectively.

Once, I listened to some young film-makers: "Well, we can shoot more. Let's pop that. We'll cut that in. Hey, why don't we shoot that? That's good."

"Hey, we've still got another eight hundred feet."

"Okay, let's shoot his big toe."

Better that film be left in the magazine to rot forever than to grind it indiscriminately. Inevitably it will be cut in, one way or another. Freedom becomes license, and license, in this case, becomes excess film.

I shoot quite a bit of material, usually coming in at around a hundred and ten thousand feet, pretty close to ten to one—ten feet of film for every foot I use in the finished film. That average has been consistent in the seventeen pictures I've directed. Yet I'm not consciously aware of footage amounts on a day-by-day basis. It can run from Los Angeles to Chicago. What counts is what is on the film.

Basically it is against the instincts of every good cinematographer, camera operator or director to move the camera simply for the sake of moving it. The same thing prevails with delivery. It is one of the director's most vital tools. In my case, there are thirty ways to show a joke—insert it, cut to it, refer to it, punch it, lay back, double-cut! But why, and how?

George Marshall and I did a joke in *Hook, Line and Sinker*. We were doing a progression of scenes where a poor married man is getting his bellyful of domestic crap— weeding the plants, washing his car, sweating a broken garbage disposal. In this montage of annoyances we have The Idiot, the husband, painting on a ladder. The top of it is out of frame. The kids and dog run through the patio and knock it over. George was prepared to cut to The Idiot on his ass, paint all over him.

It was against my chemistry. I said, "George, when the kids run through and we see the ladder go over, we presume they just knocked it over. Okay, let's get another cut of the kids running further with the dog, then take them about a hundred and eighty degrees running back to where they created the trouble. They jump over the ladder, we widen a hair, and we see what was on the ladder."

I got livid to think we were going to knock this thing over, then cut to something that said visually, "Oh, I was on the ladder and they knocked me off." Certainly, it would have worked with the cut. But it was better with a sweep. It delivered better with a camera movement.

Early in films there was a difficulty in orientation. People did not understand screen progression or movement: lefts and rights, exits. This caused growth of explicit travel or progression information and for a long time there was a tendency to overdo each step. Now, with audiences understanding screen technology, it is sufficient to show the female character leaving and to cut back to the male, rather than showing her actual exit and return to the male.

Stage right is the same on the sound stage as it is in the theater, but on the camera side it becomes camera left. The director is behind the camera for camera left. In crew discussions, terms should be *camera left* and *camera right*, but in instructing actors the safest method is *stage right* and *stage left* to avoid confusion.

Sooner or later, you are going to have camera operators panning right for an actor whom you told to exit stage right. Actually, it is a camera-left exit. The two sound-stage jargons, because of camera position and the ultimate projection of the film, sometimes become confusing. My problem is even greater because I am usually performing as well as directing. I put colors on the camera to simplify action for the cast. "Look at the camera and exit green, not red." The actor doesn't have to burden himself with stage or camera directions.

It is not unusual to see actors, directors, editors and cameramen who have been in the business thirty years arguing about right and left exits and entrances.

two

Post PROduction

11

EDITING

Once I walked into a cold, sleepy cutting room at four-thirty in the morning and lifted a son-of-a-bitch of a shot out of a film. Two and a half feet! I hated it with a passion. It was right for the film, right for the scene, but I hadn't shot it the right way. Even though it worked, it wasn't honest. I yanked it.

The film-maker has to learn to cut without bleeding over the moviola, attack his own work without mercy, slash favorite scenes with cold detachment. The film is made on the moviola and he is shooting simply to run his film through it. He must learn how to piece it together on that machine—forward, backward, brake it; mark the film with a grease pencil. Cut! If he is hard-ass on the stage, he must be harder-ass in the cutting room.

Usually the director is granted *first cut* of his film, the opportunity to put it together the way he sees it, and the way he shot it. The film editor, if he is good, helps the director decide how much winds up on the screen, how much on the proverbial cutting-room floor. In effect, the director should be the cutter and the film editor, man or woman, the person who technically assembles the film. Once the film is assembled, the editor should turn to the director and say, "Now, cut your film."

It is punctuation. Frames! Three frames, six frames! Frame cutting particularly works in comedy. Two extra frames spoil a joke. A joke plays great in thirty frames but you may think it will play even better in twenty-nine. Yet you don't say, "Rusty, make it twenty-nine." Simply, you hit that break and mark it. It works on the moviola but bombs on the big screen. Back to the bench and put four frames on; take six off, add three. Try again!

In *The Bellboy*, when The Kid steals the plane, we cut the sequence thirty times before finally deciding to drop two frames. The sequence was in the hotel manager's office. The camera was positioned about ten feet from him, holding the desk and a secretary. The manager receives a phone call.

"Yes, hello. Stanley, the bellboy? Yes, he works for me. Yes."

The camera is moving slowly up to the desk, choking the manager. As it stops, he says, "He *what?*"

Before the *t* is out of his mouth, we straight cut to the Douglas DC-8 jet taking off. *Bwwwwwwooooh!*

We had a couple of frames too many.

"He *what?*" Then four frames, then the jet-engine roar. Out came two frames, and then the *bwwwwwwoooh* was on the manager's *t*. It was that critical.

I give my editor as much creative respect as I give my cinematographer. When he is better than I am, deals with my film in such a way that it rises above the design, I'm wise to leave it that way. He has saved my life a dozen times.

However, when I'm right, or when it is the exact way I want it, right or wrong: "That's the cut, Rusty. Mark it." There is no discussion.

He marks it and I watch him make the physical cut on the moviola. "Now, let's review it and move on to the next cut." If I'm wrong, I may sit at the moviola and hit the brake until my hand comes off.

Finally he'll say quietly, "Would you like me to fix it?"

"Fix it, shmuck, it's eleven-thirty at night."

Film editors do not get their jobs by going to parties at Zanuck's house. They get them because they have a story sense on film in addition to the technical applications, and because they can satisfy a director. The young film-maker can do himself a considerable favor by latching on to a good editor.

Rusty was my assistant editor when I began to direct *Bellboy* in 1960. His career grew as mine grew and, finally, I made him a full editor. While this type of association, based on friendship as well as professional respect, is not unique in the industry, it is the most productive. Few film editors are under contract to a particular director, company or studio. They change directors as their assignments change.

Under my setup, Rusty's work often begins during the initial planning of the film. It extends to the day we deliver the print to the releasing organization. During production, his 7:30 A.M. set visits start a long day that will include editing work, ordering of reprints or opticals, and assembling of the dailies. It ends with the screening of the dailies after the company wrap.

At the screening, also attended by the cinematographer, wardrobe and make-up, he may recommend: "Get one more pop of the girl. It will help us speed the material." Sometimes such a recommendation will point up dialogue that can be eliminated, which in turn eliminates the need for the protective shot. It can be edited on the script page and almost camera-cut.

Throughout production he is attempting to assemble the film on the basis of what he believes I want to see. He takes notes and often talks into a tape recorder: "He [Lewis] wants to use camera A, or 'A' angle. I don't agree but if he wants it that way . . ." Eventually the moviola or the screen itself will say who is right or wrong.

As he goes along, Rusty makes a list of what he calls garbage. As I cut the film and pull the garbage out, he checks the list. At the end of nine, ten or eleven weeks, he refers back to the list: "There's still a piece of garbage left." I either keep it or dump it. Most important, I've been told it's there.

In viewing the assembled sequences, still in a rough cut, I may find he stayed too long on the master or didn't go to the close pieces on the impact. He makes the changes and we run again in a day or two. Assembling on a daily basis throughout the filming period, he has the rough cut or sometimes a fairly smooth cut by the time shooting is completed.

If the director is good, his first cut is often close to what the talented film editor would deliver if he had total freedom. He wants nothing more than to have the director give him that first cut. He can go home early. But if the director's first cut is bad, and he's taken off the film by the studio, then the producer may dictate the new changes. After that, the executive producer can butt in with his ideas. Finally, the studio committee, the front-office execs, put in their two pennies of thought. Before it's over, the poor editor has gone through four or five cuts, all different from the first. He suffers and the film suffers.

The director's first cut should be gold. No one can do it for him because no one else can truly get into his mind. If he doesn't know how to make that first cut, he really doesn't know how to shoot the movie. Unless it all comes down to the moviola, masters, singles, over-ons, tonality of scenes and attitudes of actors, there is no reason for him to be assigned. When a studio takes a film away from a director it is usually a sign that he shouldn't have been hired in the first place.

Highly creative top directors like Joe Mankiewicz still read books on film editing. They read them, reread them, then toss them away because of the preponderance of nonsense in them. The only place to learn film editing is in the cutting room, sitting at the moviola or standing behind the cutter's high swivel chair, watching the emulsion fly by.

At the same time, unfortunately, the strong director who has a thorough grasp of his racket may creatively stifle the film editor. He may reduce him to a simple mechanic, little more than an assembler of film. If the editor happens to be talented and creative, such handling is ultimately the film's loss. The loss is in balance and objectivity.

The director should know, up to a point, the technical aspects of opticals. He should have an understanding of dissolves, flips and fades. But his own judgment in timing will serve as much as a wide technical knowledge. He won't order an eight-foot dissolve in, and eight out, if he wants the scene transition to be quick. He'll order three in, and three out. There is a hard application of common sense to many of the technicalities.

✿   ✿   ✿

Sometimes the director will be too critical of his own work. On occasion I find myself being supercritical. Invariably I'll turn to my editor when I'm in that kind of self-imposed trap. He'll usually suggest I table the cuts and look at them a week later.

I suppose the true test of objectivity is in the cutting room. Of course, it is even tougher to be objective when you've directed yourself around the stage. Then it is: "Rusty, dump him. I did something wrong with him." I think I have dumped more of Jerry Lewis than any other actor. He's very sad when he's not funny. There have been times when I had to keep him, funny or not, because of my own mistakes on the set.

Eventually there comes a time when a wrap must be called in the cutting room, when the product has to be shipped. No one can play with it endlessly. It is a lovely yet maddening last act. Usually the director wishes he could get the goddamn thing back and re-cut it. No way! It is already in the theaters.

Years later I've re-cut pictures, as have many other directors. I've done it simply for personal satisfaction.

12

MUSIC AND DUBBING

After the film goes through its tortures in the cutting room, with a little of the director's heart, blood and dreams strewn over the floor midst the trims, a ceremony called "cue"-ing takes place. The final rough-cut film is run, reel by reel, in a projection room with equipment that will reverse as well as run forward. Often a sequence must be repeated for a second look. A large illuminated counter indicates the footage, and the film is backed up to the desired point, then run forward again.

Gathered at this session are the principal post-production workers. They include the director, his editor, the composer, the music cutters, the sound-effects team and sometimes special photographic-effects technicians. In large studios, the post-production department heads will also attend. Few other sessions are as important as "cue"-ing. It is one of the next to final steps toward completion of the film.

At this stage it is likely that the opticals, the dissolves and fades, have not been cut in, but the editor's grease marks on the film, visible on the screen, indicate the lengths. It enables the conposer and sound-effects cutters to time their needs.

As a total film-maker I personally cue all my films, indicating where the music should be and what type it should be. More important, I indicate areas that should not be scored. It is flexible, of course, and often a decision is made to score a sequence that had been planned to play without music. During this session I talk into a tape recorder so the composer has a verbal guide for later transcription.

Simultaneously the sound-effects cutter is noting the effects needed at a given footage. The roar of a car may need augmenting; a realistic-sounding gunshot may have to be *laid in* on his effects track. Weather sounds, such as wind, the crack of lightning, or rain, may have to be added. Other sounds in the original recorded track may have to be *sweetened*, or intensified. A tape-recorder guide is also made for him and later transcribed, "cue"-ing his work according to the reel-and-footage counter.

A number of sound-effects tracks are "built" for each film, reel by reel, and blended with the dialogue and music tracks, in synchronization with the picture at the *dubbing* session. There they are blended into one master sound track—a combination of dialogue, effects and music.

The director has to know what he wants to hear in his score, and the shortest route to convey the desired sound is to use facsimiles. I often stop at Music City, a large music store in Hollywood, to pick up pieces of music I've heard and want to relate to a film. They have the mood I think is needed for certain parts of the upcoming score.

For example, I have an idea of what I think I want for music behind the main title. So I buy a piece of temporary material that is very close to what I would like. Or I obtain it, in some cases, from the studio's music library. I have it *traced*, or copied, and actually use that music while I shoot the main title. After scoring, the new and final piece of music, which has the same mood of the temporary track, is laid in. Using variations of this method, I also find it helpful to score the film as I go along. The temporary material is a guide to pace and feeling.

If there is pantomime a temporary music track can perform magic on the stage during filming. Camera, movement and players are all locked into the music. The sync is there; the feel is there; the tone is there. As with the main title, the temporary music is lifted and the composer duplicates it with his own version. This is still another example of tracing.

In scenes other than pantomime, music can be effective for setting mood for the actors. A ninety-dollar Sony tape player, cracked down just enough for the actors to hear it but not enough for the directional mike to pick up, is sufficient. Of course, it sometimes throws an actor. It is a sound foreign to him. Scratch the music! It isn't worth ruining the scene.

Long before the composer is signed, during homework and during filming, the director should be thinking of music for his picture—gathering ideas for sequences he believes will need scoring. He should also be thinking about the type of composer that will be best for the picture.

One way or another, the composer must *hear* what the director wants. It is difficult to explain it other than in a musical form. For example, I will play a temporary track over a scene of people walking in a bus station, then tell the composer, "Write that music."

"But we aren't allowed to use that!"

"So, compose your own but don't change anything."

He will change some things but he has *heard* the music. Words won't do it.

Music should not frighten the new film-maker. It is not that complicated. I am not a professional musician, but with Walter Scharf wrote a song for *The Bellboy*, using the first five notes of "The Star-Spangled Banner." It became the theme for the whole film. Of course, this way of working with music is the exception and not the rule. Yet it is productive, and an additional tool.

The decision on when to score and when to exclude music is the director's choice, not the composer's. Each film is guided by different applications of music. The guidelines are in the scenes. The scene either cries for a musical treatment or it literally begs the director to exclude it. If there is doubt about scoring a scene, the safest way is to score it. It can always be dialed out in dubbing.

One of the most difficult things in handling music is overlapping. The director has to constantly remember the next scene to avoid carrying a three-minute piece, for example, into the top of the next sequence. Again, a temporary track is the best solution.

When working with an experienced, professional composer, the director will get what he wants nine times out of ten. A chase has to be covered in a certain way; a comedy scene should be scored in one sequence, excluded in another. Mickey Mouse music—high note, low note, higher note—can be used when a man picks up a cigarette and then drops it. There are occasions in comedy when the score should oppose the funny action rather than complement it.

Eventually, reel by reel, the composer knows what the director wants and then hides away six to eight weeks to write the score. The individual pieces may run only a few seconds. Or three or four minutes. Then the orchestra is hired, and he conducts his new score to the individual scenes projected on the screen on the scoring stage. He sees the film, times to it, although he has already timed it according to the footage count, reel for reel.

For *Hook, Line and Sinker* I had over sixty minutes of

music with a full orchestra. In one scoring session alone we recorded twenty-six minutes of music. For a comedy, it was a musically "heavy" picture. Other films might not have more than twenty minutes including the main title. The musical needs of each film vary.

A director with a thorough knowledge of his film can hear music on the composer's piano before the orchestra is ever called and make judgment. I have done that on occasions when the composer was not clear about the needs. I have also "sung" an idea for him to record and then return with a rough composition. This rarely happens because the screen material should speak for itself.

After a "cue"-ing session a composer might say, "Well, there's a piece of material in the second reel that I'd like to score . . ."

The idea can be rejected, but it is usually wise to permit the extra scoring. If it doesn't work, it can be dialed out in dubbing. But the composer's extra piece can also turn out to be a hit. This is another time when creativity can be easily destroyed by offhand rejection. The composer-director relationship, one of the final creative associations in a film, should be an extension of the sound-stage humanities. Let him go his way and very often you'll get some great things you never thought about.

Whether comedy, drama, love story or western, everyone tries for a hit song. It can be from the main title, the central musical theme, or simply a song within the picture. It has the potential of selling the film, adding thousands, even hundreds of thousands, at the box office. If it becomes an Academy Award song, it could add a million to the gross receipts.

The "Pink Panther" theme sold thousands of dollars in tickets for that film, and "Raindrops Are Fallin' " did the same for *Butch Cassidy and The Sundance Kid.* The "Colonel Bogey March" from *River Kwai* is a classic example.

A hit song or theme should be sought after just as avidly as a hit film. Worldwide, radio is a much larger selling market than television. Additionally, TV commercial time is too expensive for film-exploitation saturation. A hit song from a film on the radio provides what amounts to a free ride for the distribution company. Disc jockeys usually identify it with the film.

Obviously the main-title treatment, or the song treatment within the film, should not distract from the story simply in hopes of a hit song. If the title is animated and animation is a story point, then lyrics should not burden it. Audiences find it hard to digest sight and sound if too much is going on.

If the film is a *Barefoot in the Park,* where the main-title theme can project through to the story, both objectives can be realized. With *Pink Panther* and its main-title treatment, lyrics would have been confusing. If it is a James Bond picture, there are no rules for treatment. As with all other phases of film-making, each story requires different handling of themes and songs.

I have a theory that the key to dubbing a film successfully, achieving the composite sound track, is deletion. It's done, of course, at the studio, in a large soundproofed room with a half dozen guys seated before rows of dials. Each of these sound mixers have several tracks, music or sound effects, to blend together with the dialogue track in exact synchronization with the film.

The sound-effects cutters always tend to go overboard. They cover every possible sound in the film, from a door squeak to a volcano blowing its top, and sometimes go Mickey Mouse with them. In the dubbing room, with the picture playing on a screen in front of the mixing panels, a scratching of the head sometimes sounds like lightning and thunder.

Or there might be a door with a small knocker in one scene. The door slams. You hear *ch-ka-ka!* What? On the screen you're already cutting away as the door slams. The audience doesn't even see the knocker. Delete one *ch-ka-ka!* It takes hours to get the superfluous sound-effects garbage dialed out.

With music, you are swelling it for dramatic effect, or softening it; sometimes entirely deleting material, or making *cross-overs*, joining two pieces of music. If the music is clocked down to thirty-seven and seven-tenths seconds, and the scene plays thirty-four and seven-tenths, you obviously have three seconds for the cross-over. You dial it out, or let it play through the dissolve. If you are in a six-foot dissolve, then the music comes out at the dead-center point, with the incoming music crossing over. If there is no incoming music, it can be played out through the dissolve.

In the final analysis, the film-maker's ears are his expertise in the dubbing room. He doesn't need to know the dials or what plugs into where. He knows his film, and knows what sounds he wants to hear. A quarter dropping into an empty dishpan makes only one sound. Add water to it and it makes another sound. The engineer might say, "I was there. I put the quarter up here and kicked it off and it fell into the pan. There is no water!"

"Bull-shit! Now, get me what I want. Go out and record a quarter falling into a washpan without any water in it."

With the normal hearing God gave him, the film-maker must fight his way through the dubbing room demanding what sounds right to his ears.

13

DISTRIBUTION AND EXPLOITATION

You made your deal; you made the picture! You stood outside a theater and saw the lines at the box office. Then the accounting comes in from the distribution company and you yell, "Where does the money go?"

Well, between shipping the finished print to New York and its release in the theaters there is that painful, costly process called distribution. And distribution is part of exhibition. And the accounting is a part of both.

"Ah, Mr. Lewis, we thought you wanted to go three hundred thousand with the exploitation," says Distribution.

"Yes, but not six hundred and ten thousand. Where does that figure come from?"

"Well, ah, we can get to the figures Monday."

"No! Now! What Monday? You picked up three hundred and ten thousand of my money so swift I couldn't see it happen. But now it's going to take you four days to see the numbers. Why aren't you as fast to show me where it is as you were to take it? Sir, do I have to call an audit?"

I recently called an audit on some of my pictures. One studio sent a check for $171,000. The envelope hadn't hit the basket before my attorney had them on the phone: "There's one hundred and twenty-seven thousand dollars missing!"

They said, "We'll get back to you."

They got back in a few days, oozing syrup: "Do you know something? That's one of the first times we've made that glaring an error."

Their answer is always, "Ooops!" They give you a friggin' gun to put to your temple. But I told the attorney, "I don't want the money. Send back the initial check. Tell them I want to challenge them now. If they made that kind of error there has to be more."

They have an excuse for every challenge. The film-maker cannot damage the studio because they stole money. Suddenly the money is a gift—found money. Whatever money is recovered "is money no longer coming to the film-maker." They are mentally geared to operate this way, structured to operate in this manner.

Yet I don't believe they think that their operation is dishonest. The structure is so huge that the theft becomes part of the total concept. There is no board chairman who will stand up and say, "Last year we beat people for a million three . . ." It just happens within the structure. But they get livid when they are challenged because they aren't aware they are stealing.

On the lower echelons the theft is more open—that expense-account item for the publicity putz in New York: "I took her to dinner for forty-two dollars. I'll mark the voucher sixty-eight." That is known, and unbeatable, but the large amounts—a half million dollars on a picture with sixteen more to follow in the release pattern—is structured theft. It is allowed theft.

One of Sam Goldwyn's more famous stories came out of *Guys and Dolls,* starring Frank Sinatra and Marlon Brando. In making the deal with Sinatra, the agent wanted X number of dollars. Goldwyn replied, "I could give him that much money because he is Frank Sinatra, but because of what the distributors are going to steal from me on this picture I've got to save everywhere I can."

The studios and distribution companies are seldom really hurting. They are in the same business as the building superintendent. He lives in his flat free while the tenants pay ninety-eight a month. He is the superintendent and doesn't give a damn what you do inside the flat as long as you don't touch the walls. The studios are in the renting business, not creation.

Angry with them? Go somewhere else. You can't walk around the country with three hundred cans of film under your arm and sell to each theater individually. They have the distribution. Okay, go somewhere else.

"Well, let's go to Commonwealth. They're new."

They're also prepared for you. Get a lawyer to stand in the wings. They're new but they're already structured.

It's the old joke: "He ain't laid a glove on you." "Well, watch the referee. Someone's kicking the shit out of me."

There are a few places to watch, mainly the exploitation columns. Paid advertising for radio, television, newspaper space; publicity costs. The film-maker can indicate how much he wants to spend, and then look for the play time of his ads. He can monitor them to a degree.

Recently I stopped blank-check invoices for my company. I wrote the distributor: "Don't send me an invoice with twelve newspapers listed. I want to see *which* newspapers, and attached to the invoice the lines per invoice."

That wiped them out, freaked them. "Well, we just can't do that."

I phoned Publicity and Advertising: "I'll tell you what I'll do. I'll send a man to New York. He'll sit in your offices, paid by me. As you order the material, he'll follow it up. You just send the individual dual invoice. He'll send the attachments."

They got nice! Quick! I wound up getting an invoice for sixteen dollars in stamps. Even then, they beat me. The actual purchase was for eight dollars.

The film-maker must help sell his product. An involvement in publicity is necessary. Once again, there are few secrets. Publicity can be learned by instinct. The film-maker should know how he wants his product presented to the public, and will usually recognize the wrong approach to that selling.

I start a publicity-and-advertising campaign, or at least the approach to it, before the film goes into production. On the average, my publicity and advertising costs, worldwide, run about $290,000 for each $2 million film. It is not a lot of money in terms of the production budget and probably below the average spent on films with similar budgets. But it cannot be figured in percentages. The film-maker must decide what he wants for his campaign, and how much he can afford.

The publicity and ad departments of the studios begin thinking about the campaign after reading the script. Very often, after finishing a script, I will write ideas for the campaign based solely on the new story. Then a meeting is held with the exploitation people, in Hollywood or New York. I offer my ideas as to what can be done with it. Occasionally, I go to a non-studio artist and have him render ad ideas for presentation to the home office in New York.

Sometimes the publicity or ad staffs will read the comic portion of the script and ignore the "something" to say. Or they go off half-cocked on the whole thing. Further explanation is required.

"Yeah, we've got it now, Jer. Right!"

Two months later, the ad concepts are shipped from New York. It looks like another show, not mine at all. "Where did you get the dirty broad with the bazooms hanging out. She's not in my picture."

So I have to fly to New York, patiently sit with the guys again or show them a piece of film. That is the ideal way, of course, to present the film. There is little difference in the functions of the publicity and advertising departments, from one distribution company to another. It is largely a matter of the film-maker having patience, then pushing, and finally demanding.

In writing a script, I'm always aware of the publicity potentials. If the joke involves a kitchen and all the tools in the kitchen, it can be just as funny, or funnier, done in the grand-ballroom kitchen of the Hilton Hotel. There is also the bonus of a Hilton publicity or advertising tie-up. I did this in one film. There were no verbal plugs, just the visual of "Hilton." In exchange, the film received thousands of dollars in free exploitation.

A joke might work beautifully with a big funny-looking Mercedes-Benz. But Mr. M. Benz couldn't care less about having his car shown in any film. He won't give a dime for a movie-advertising tie-up. So the car is changed to a Lincoln-Continental and the tie-up is made. For five straight years I wrote a Rolls-Royce into scripts but never heard from them.

During my last film, twenty to thirty products came across my desk, each available for use if I could write them in. I used a few. No money is exchanged, and they aren't listed in the credits. They are visible on the screen, and in return, the companies guarantee magazine ad space or television time. The products cannot be plugged because the TV people will delete them when the film is sold to the networks.

Still pictures offer another tie-in exploitation for a film: "Bob Hope rides United Airlines." For one film, I did a still for Interwoven socks. That company spent seven hundred thousand for ads, plugging the film in each one. It was considerably more than the entire distribution-company-ad budget for the film's exploitation. It is a big plus in today's marketing of a film.

The payola issue has died a justified death. It started with writers and I was guilty of it, along with many writers in the industry. Under-the-table payments were made for use or mention of a product on the screen. Now it is above board, and contracts are drawn up between the manufacturing or sales company and the production companies.

Not long ago I went to Portugal to direct some sequences in Lisbon. I used Trans-World Airlines in all the scenes involving flight. TWA paid for this exploitation, as opposed to some companies which exchange this type of cooperation for ad mentions.

While working with the writer on the second *Salt and Pepper* script, I was approached one morning by the producer. "Can you arrange for this whole flight to take place on BOAC? They'll give us forty round-trip fares!" Why not? Cash value of those fares amounts to at least $40,000. If Mexicana Airlines wants to make a deal, we'll fly by way of Mexico City. Again, why not? *However, no tie-up should hurt the story-line or the production values of the film.* No amount of exploitation is worth that.

In-flight films, the 16 mm jet projections over martinis and macadamia nuts, offer healthy revenues at present. I made one film that American Airlines wanted to buy for exhibition at thirty-eight thousand feet, but there was a TWA sequence in it. It was a $25,000 deal.

I got the negative back, and on a Sunday eliminated three hundred feet from the second master, then ground out twelve prints for American Airlines with TWA missing. It cost five thousand to make the deletions but earned an eventual profit of twenty.

14

OTHER FILM-MAKERS, OTHER FILMS

Fellini said, "There are no other film-makers. When I am making a film, that is the only film there is. I couldn't be interested in another man's work. It would take my mind off mine. I would be depriving my baby of its nourishment and I don't want to clap my hands for another man's work."

After reading that, I felt less guilty about missing a lot of films that should be examined by today's young film-maker. When I'm involved with a film, which is a rather constant process, I have no time to see the other man's work. I don't even have a desire to see it. Yet the new director, or new writer, must examine the other works of film, and not follow Fellini's diet.

"I'm convinced that the best example of a total film-maker was Chaplin. He was totally in, on, and all over his films. He created them in the fullest sense of the word: experimented to see how widely, how cleverly and skillfully he could work.

Chaplin also had a powerful family of fine comic people who worked with him picture after picture. He often used one actor for three different roles within the same film, changing costume and make-up to change characters. Ford Sterling played three completely different roles in *City Lights*. Once he was in a wheel-chair, then up on a perch; for another sequence, in an envelope.

Chaplin saw actors as people, then as dramatic tools. They performed for him that way. He made the statement that Marlon Brando's casting in *Countess from Hong Kong* was because of Brando's lack of humor. It implies that Chaplin believed he would have comic control over Brando if he played the straight man. His lack of ability as a comedian was an asset. There were scenes when Brando moved like a puppet. The picture went haywire, but Chaplin's planning was correct.

Countess from Hong Kong, which should have had gentler treatment from the critics, went haywire because of time. Just after seeing it I watched a TV documentary on Jesse Owens, the champion runner. There were shots of him running in the Berlin Olympic Games of 1936 and shots of him walking in 1968. His walk from just one spot to another was frightening. He'd atrophied.

The same thing happened to Charlie Chaplin. He made *Modern Times* in 1936 and *Countess* in 1967. He hadn't been given the opportunity to stay alive creatively because of the leftist issue. Thirty-one years after *Modern Times*, Chaplin was tackling the same problems in a wholly different world with a different speed, different people— different juices. There was no way for his creative mind to cook.

Sophia Loren? She'd better have the chauffeured car in Pasadena or she won't do the film in Rome. Why? "That's what she wants! She gets it!"

So Loren walks on the set and confronts Mr. Brando with his cooking juices. Plus Chaplin's wife sitting around hoping he doesn't croak from a coronary; eight children running around tripping the grips. This beautiful little man faced devastation for his last film.

But the older men like Chaplin and Hitchcock were masters of their craft during their prime years. They were great artists with people and with the tools of their art. George Stevens, in directing *A Place in the Sun, Giant* and *The Greatest Story Ever Told*, shows mastery in almost every frame. Each picture is beautifully textured; everything grooves. They are expertly tailored, and the viewer, whether or not he enjoys the film or the subject matter, is unconsciously aware of the fine stitching throughout. Certainly, Stevens overshoots, but *Giant* was not a matter of luck or accident.

I respect Hitchcock and his superb talents but hate some of his films. I hated *Psycho*, although it was a good movie. He crossed the line of decency. Nor do I want to be that frightened by a film. After seeing it at the DeMille Theater in New York I went to a bar and shook a brandy down. I couldn't enter the bathroom in the hotel without shuddering.

Next time I saw Hitchcock I told him what I thought. He agreed. He said, "Yes, I agree with you. I think it's terrible. It made a fortune." Although that statement sounds facetious, I think Hitch deep down did not like the film because of the degree to which he went. In the stabbing of Marty Balsam coming up the steps, the shock exceeded the act, i.e. Janet Leigh in the shower.

The work of a Fred Zinnemann comes from knowledge, care and lots of sweat. Films like *High Noon, The Sundowners* and *A Man for All Seasons* are the product of a master craftsman. Any young director can learn quite a lesson by watching what he did with the camera, how he handled the actors and treated the subject matter as the result of both.

The director has the opportunity of helping the actor get the most out of his material. Film after film, Kirk Douglas is a fine and powerful actor. Rarely is his potential reached. In *Lust for Life*, Vincente Minnelli touched his heart. Playing Van Gogh, of course, offers the material potential but Minnelli hits a special chord to soften Douglas. He took his heart.

Not long ago I talked with Paul Newman. He is in full bloom of masculine manhood, but he is also nine years old. He has a blowgun, balloons, firecrackers. He is nasty and quick-tempered, selfish and self-centered. He is also terribly kind, warm and generous. He is incensed, for instance, that the late Dr. Oppenheimer gave the last information to blow up Hiroshima. Simply, he is very human.

We were talking about *Cool Hand Luke* and Stuart Rosenberg, the director. I wanted to hear Newman's explanation of a good director. Paul said, "When Rosenberg talked to me, I knew what it was to be special." Newman's performance in *Cool Hand Luke,* on a par with his role in *Somebody Up There Likes Me,* is proof of that feeling of *being special.*

Oddly enough, very few seasoned actors can explain why a certain director is a fine director. Yet, repeatedly, the candidates for the list of best directors have one thing in common—the solid human factor.

Why is Marlon Brando so magnificent in *The Wild Ones, Desiree* and *On the Waterfront* and so miserable in *Mutiny on the Bounty*? What happened to Brando? It was the same Brando, with the same talents, the same capabilities.

Nothing happened to *him.* There was a magic that did not happen. Lewis Milestone, the *Mutiny* director, could not confer with this troubled child. Elia Kazan knew

Brando and had made him the giant of the industry in *On the Waterfront*. Kazan sat him down with Rod Steiger, another child who was not very troubled. But Kazan knew how to make Mr. Brando aware that the other child did not need the same cares and concerns.

In making *Funny Girl*, William Wyler permitted Barbra Streisand to take control of the film: tell him where to put the lights, which side of her face to photograph. I could not do that. I am not that good as yet. I'd rather vomit than have a member of my cast direct the film.

Wyler is a great director, has integrity and a deep regard for his own talent. Until Barbra Streisand, no actor or actress had ever advised Mr. Wyler what to do. Speaking of the experience, Wyler told me that he enjoyed working with her and that she knew herself better than he ever would. She does have tremendous talent, and knows what she needs, but what came up on the screen in *Funny Girl*, a very successful picture, was Wyler's. *She* didn't get it up there. *He* was the heavyweight, and used his own methods to achieve it; she's magnificent, but so is he!

Robert Wise, a fine director, lost control working with Julie Andrews in *Star*, and/or dropped the ball, which is quite understandable in that I think he became so enamored of the "star" who enveloped his whole creative being that the result wound up being much less than it should have been.

I've never seen Wise move a camera like that: set shots; walk out, walk in; left right, right left—such static material

in the first three reels that I didn't even eat my Nestlé's
Crunch. I loved Gertie Lawrence, liked Julie Andrews and
think Wise is a terrific director, yet ended the night with
angry disappointment. It was all a toast, a very expensive
one, to Julie Andrews.

Sound of Music, produced and directed by Wise, was a
marvelous film. Sit through it, enjoy it. Nothing static. I
think it is a good example of the emulsion capturing the
feeling and attitude of the film-maker and stars. It smelled
of lilacs and roses, and Miss Andrews obviously respected
the material. It is also obvious, in comparing the two films,
that Wise had stronger feelings about *Sound of Music.* He
projected the loveliness and enchantment of the stage musical.

Star smacks of the director's loss of control. The audience cannot relate to it. They cannot relate to Julie Andrews as Gertrude Lawrence. At times it sounded as if
other material might be there, but Julie was saying silently,
"You can't say that, you can't say that." At a cost of more
than $10 million it bombed to the point that 20th Century
–Fox changed the title and re-released it. It fared no better. Make *enough* films, even if you are Robert Wise, and
you'll bomb once in a while.

There are many directors not in the category of a Robert
Wise, a William Wyler, a George Stevens or a Zinnemann
who turn out fine pictures and may someday do their classic. Norman Jewison, Larry Peerce, Artie Penn and Ralph
Nelson are in that category. Nelson generates a special

kind of excitement, but he carries it beyond vitality and energy. He seeks out solid material, then pours in vitality. That intangible something of making a film his way soon creates excitement.

John Cassavetes is another director, not nearly as established as Nelson, who will break through. He is more concerned about film-making than making a name for himself. Considering the conditions in which he had to work, *Shadows* was a good film. He made the *Too Late Blues* at Paramount and it failed, although it had some marvelous things in it. Capable of creating excitement, Cassavetes is an exceptional film-maker and I think *Faces* proves it; *Husbands* is another story.

A huge error is made by many of the hopeful young directors. They gorge themselves on a diet of vogue films. They see Fellini and Godard. They see *Easy Rider, The Graduate, In Cold Blood,* and sometimes, reluctantly, a *Guess Who's Coming to Dinner.* They wouldn't be caught in disguise going into the El Ray on Wilshire to see *Holiday in Bermuda.* But it is just as important to buy the El Ray ticket, or see *Flicka Goes to Sweden,* if Universal ever made that one, as it is to see *Midnight Cowboy.*

Each one has information. If the film student can fight off sleep and wait for the midnight car commercial with the friggin' dog, he will discover some wonderful things. He can steal from them. More important, he will see things to avoid—exits camera right and cuts that were made with pinking shears. There are a lot of crummy films loaded with information that can't be bought. The worst "B" picture is an education.

Ninety percent of the avant-garde clique who proclaim, "Look at the greatness of his film," are ashamed to admit they don't know what the hell it is all about. They can't wait to run to the coffeehouse to breathe out, "Wasn't that magnificent?"

God forbid someone asks, "What did it mean?"

There's a long silence. Then some creep with a beard and thick lenses says, "What's the difference?"

Fellini can provide a fine hour and a half of entertainment but teaches very little. The only way to really learn from Fellini would be to sleep with him, hear him think, and then see his product. In contrast, the old school of film-making is highly educational because nothing is hidden behind innuendos. There is no debate about inner meanings. You know the guy has the hots for a broad the minute they come to the close-up.

Critics raved about the subliminal cuts in *The Pawnbroker*. They were unique. They made the film, adding a special "different" to it. Yet many people did not understand them. I watched some of the audience trying to figure out what they meant. Though it was a fine film in every way, *The Pawnbroker* distracted a percentage of its audience with the eye-blink cuts.

Should the newcomer decide to copy *The Pawnbroker*'s subliminal cutting (if he has the luxury of preparation, time and work that must go into it), he should also be aware that the broad, general audience may not accept it. Sidney Lumet made his film for a select audience.

A Man and a Woman did not play in Fort Wayne, Indiana, for the same reasons that *Blow-up* did not play there. *A Man and a Woman* did not play theatrically in many areas of America simply because it wouldn't be understood or accepted. Chopped up, it could reach television, but a *Beverly Hillbillies* would outdraw it.

If the young film-maker decides to go after the widest possible audience he uses *Sound of Music* as the guideline; for select audiences, *The Pawnbroker*. Both should be made, but it is seldom that he will be able to move from one to the other. A harsher fact is that the studios and distribution companies, while making snotty noises about distinguished, limited-appeal films, don't want them.

Insofar as an eight-hour Andy Warhol film is concerned, I lump the avant-garde and the underground in the category of *film users* rather than film-makers. Often they are using film indulgently for no other purpose than to create controversy. Some will achieve a minimal art-house following, but few will go beyond it.

Want to be avant-garde, make 10.1 zoom hand-held moves; use a fish-eye lens on a lady and distort her so she looks like Lon Chaney's ass; lose dimension, dump the focus, and be like François Truffaut? By all means, do it! But first, find out about a 35 mm aperture, with a crab dolly, and a boom man. Truffaut gathered all the ordinary information, then threw it all away to make film.

Some young film-makers say they'll venture across the pond and join the Europeans to do their stories. Make like Godards or Fellinis. Perhaps the magic will rub off; perhaps the Godard flavor will seep into the emulsion. The chances are slim. They'll simply end up making cheap American films in Europe.

While watching both *The Pawnbroker* and a *Guess Who's Coming to Dinner*, observing a Sidney Lumet as well as a Stanley Kramer, the start has to be made in the minors. And there is a great deal to be said for the training in broad family-entertainment films with their simple approaches to the A, B and C of the camera and its utilization.

It is intriguing and useful to listen to the sacred rhetoric of cinema groups and intellectual critics, but very little of it gets up on the screen in the next picture.

three

15

LAUGHS ARE OUR THING

I had seven hundred and thirty-five young people who wanted to join a comedy workshop. The audition was very simple. I asked them why they wanted to do comedy.

First, a few negative responses:

"Well, I want to do comedy because I want to give to the world . . ."

"I want to give to the world. There are a lot of people who can't walk who should laugh a lot."

The ones who made it said:

"I want to do comedy because something in here is chewing away at me."

"I want to do comedy because I don't know why."

Maybe, for some of us, after we cut away the drivel, comedy is our bag because it is in our gut. We have no choice. It's laugh or cry. Laughs are our thing. People can't hate when they are laughing.

A good comedian, I think, comes from a shallow beginning if not a minority group. Shallow emotionally or financially, often both. No one from a silver-spoon family has ever been a top banana. A few have tried but haven't made it.

Comedy, humor, call it what you may, is often the difference between sanity and insanity, survival and disaster, even death. It's man's emotional safety valve. If it wasn't for humor, man could not survive emotionally. Peoples who have the ability to laugh at themselves are the peoples who eventually make it. Blacks and Jews have the greatest senses of humor simply because their safety valves have been open so long.

Humor works in strange ways, always close to the pulses of life. Sometimes there is a smile or a laugh of disbelief when misfortune is reported. Then hysteria breaks. Often a weird laugh can be heard at a funeral. It is either to protect a sob or because of an inability to sob. In funeral processions, jokes about the dead person are defenses against the tragedy. Many times, comedy plays directly off tragedy.

I've always felt that comedy is reality. What isn't real isn't identifiable; man only laughs when he identifies. If the comedic form is not reality in its purest sense, it often becomes a caricature of reality. Comedy is never fantasy, although fantasy can be comedic. Pure fantasy is seldom genuinely funny because it stands as an entity in itself.

Identification, and identification alone, is what makes comedy work. If the punch line of an American joke is delivered in Swedish to an American audience, you won't hear a thistle drop. Comedy does not need to be verbal, of course. Anyone can identify with the fat man who drops his ice-cream cone on taking the first lick. But if it is verbal, it must be understood for identification.

I'm deeply committed to comedy because it is in my gut. I also feel there is nothing more dramatic than comedy. So there is no purpose in my doing a non-comic film. There are too few comedians in a troubled world, and why make it one less for the questionable compensation of joining the effete ranks at the Screen Directors' Guild? I am dedicated to comedy film-making because of my gut needs and because I know it best.

When I speak of my own comedy, as a performer, I often refer to the "nonsense I make." I do it with pride and affection and not in a self-derogatory way. I am nine years old when performing comedy. At that age, hurt is possible but degradation is seldom possible.

Some actors, unable to understand comedy, look upon it as less than dignified. I've worked with them and cast them in films. They are lost causes and cannot be taught crying and happy, in ten minutes or ten years. They don't know what they are missing.

Comedy has the reward of universality and the reaction of a different warmth. If Paul Newman walks down the street, women may go, "Oh, ho!" There is a physical attraction and certainly a warmth. But when Red Skelton walks down the same street, there is often a "Tee-heeee." A membrane in memory reminds them of a happiness he projected. Newman might have made them happy but not in the same way. They might think of Newman in terms of his last role. They think of Skelton in broad terms of laughter and happiness. It is a reward to the performer.

In Geneva not too long ago I was sitting out a mix-up in flights. Eleven or twelve Arabs were in the terminal. They are angry people. I am a Jew and my films are now banned in Jordan, Egypt and other Moslem countries. Yet they forgot their anger, forgot the war for a few minutes. Their faces lit up from old memories, films past, and I met them. It told me a great deal about people and comedy.

That same trip I was hopping around Europe on weekends: touring different factories, sometimes visiting other motion-picture studios. I crossed and recrossed the bridge of nonsense. Faces lit up. I heard laughs and calls of *"Comico,"* or whatever language applied to the country I was in. So, corn or hoke, thank God, has its lovely human rewards.

Comedy, in America at least, does not have that other sometimes dubious recompense—the award. The Academy of Motion Picture Arts and Sciences does not acknowledge comedy as such. They, as a body, look down their noses at it. So the three or four comedies that come out of Hollywood yearly are pitted against perhaps one hundred and fifty pictures in the general category.

If the comedy is subtle, and if it stars Peter Ustinov, an actor who does fairly well with the Abbey Players on occasion, they will possibly examine it. But if the writer of the *Solid Gold Cadillac*, a subtle comedy, hadn't been in the in-group, the film wouldn't have been nominated.

There is no comedy category in the Academy, but there is a technical award for Takahi Sanaki, of the Tokyo Soho Company, for his technical achievements in devising a toilet that will flush without bothering the sound mixers. There is a category for the best song written in a black-and-white musical that should have been in color but they couldn't get the stock. There is also a category for a supporting player in an original play adapted for television. TV didn't want it; the movies made it. So he has an Oscar. They also have a category for make-up.

An American in Paris was a pretty fair dancing movie. But the Academy has no dancing category. The proceeds of the big benefit went to the Academy and the Motion Picture Relief Home, but "Don't give that damn picture a category because it is all dancing . . ."

The whole smell of "Comedy, Jesus, that's low-brow" has infiltrated motion-picture-industry awards. That means, of course, the Academy. There was a film entitled *City Lights*. It was made by Mr. Chaplin. Some of the most highly regarded contemporary actors claim his performance in it is one of the finest acting jobs ever. Those who have seen it were wiped out by it. What did the Academy do? Nothing. Certain members made sure that no one pushed it for a nomination. They did not want to make waves.

When Stan Laurel had but a short time to live, pressure had to be put on the Academy for the award of a special Oscar. They might have missed him as they have missed several other now deceased masters. But not Takahi Sanaki!

It is sad that the Academy, it's members, and its governors feel this way, but then, who needs a laugh? (Note: The Keystone Kops started it *all*—why is there no category for comedy?)

For reasons unknown, critics tend to judge comedy and comedians with a harsher pen than is used for other fields of entertainment. I've been accused of not walking straight, having a hunched back and speaking with a Semitic tone in my voice. Red Skelton has been accused of having a "palsied tongue."

The comedian must become accustomed, as well as toughened, to the "uncritical criticism." He will meet it in everything he does in comedy. If he listens, he'll be wiped out and will soon be selling Florsheim shoes.

There is also a difference between the American appreciation of comedy and the foreign appreciation of it. Perhaps, in total, the Europeans are a simpler people, with a long background of wars and tragedy, crying and happy. When I go to Europe, my ego gets filled up; I am strong again because they look at comedy as the surviving fabric of life. They do not scorn it or think it is low. They can understand it and do not fret too much about being chic, digging George and Martha in *Virginia Woolf*, solely.

It is strange, and thought-provoking, that the American industry can no longer produce what literally started it: slapstick—the Keystone Kops. The studios frown on it, of course. It is not chic.

Whatever direction the industry takes in this time of change, I won't abandon comedy.

There is a classic tradition in speechmaking which has a direct relationship to comedy. It is known as the rhetoric structure: Tell the audience you are going to do something; do it; and then let them know it is done. The rule applies to comedy.

A comedian is walking boldly across a field. We see him in a knee shot, cockier than ever, but don't orient the audience to the fact that he's walking into an excavation. Dropping back to a wider shot, we see he's looking around and that his left foot is over the hole. Then to a closer cut, and he's yelling, "Ooooooh-whunk!" But until we see him flat on his ass in the excavation, the scene isn't resolved.

Laurel and Hardy used to say, "Pssst, watch this," without ever verbalizing it. It was wonderful.

"I'll ring the bell, Stanley."

There is an empty socket, and Oliver sticks his finger into it. "Eeeeeeeyoooooow!" It always came a beat before the insert shot of the finger sizzling in the socket.

The tip, the "Psssst, watch this," was a trademark of Laurel and Hardy, but it works differently with different comedians and with different film audiences. The foreign film audience likes the joke tipped hard. The American audience is more sophisticated. The foreign film viewer has the disadvantage of films subtitled in English. There are no subtitles for a visual joke, anyway.

Oddly enough, American audiences were never really aware that Laurel and Hardy were the "joke tippers" of the world. They made the rules for that technique in films, but they were so masterful there appeared to be no rule.

So the basis of all the countless variations of visual jokes is the banana peel. If the audience is not told it is there, they are busy trying to figure out what happened as the comic reacts. The thought cannot be put in their minds at the point laughter should prevail. If they have to say, or think, "Oh, it was a banana," the laugh is gone. They must laugh as the backside hits the pavement.

It is as important to punctuate a joke as it is to punctuate a point in drama or suspense. Use of the various lenses in comedy is just as necessary as it is in high drama. The same problems and benefits of camera movement apply to both. Dramatic sequences in comedy build specifically toward the punctuation of the comedy.

There is a scene in *The Nutty Professor* where this transformation from drama to comedy is clearly evident. One European critic seemed to be particularly impressed by it, and asked, "Why don't you now turn to dramatic films?" I suppose he thought I might attain greater fulfillment. It seemed to surprise him that the two had been blended successfully. But unless it is a Keystone Kop kind of comedy, the two are usually blended in all contemporary comedies.

In each film I attempt to apply substance to The Idiot's character somewhere, sometime. The serious side of his character development cannot take place early in the film. Audiences will not accept it. But once The Idiot has made them laugh, once he is communicating clearly with them on the level of laughter, he can develop substance. Audiences then not only accept it but want it. They want him to be a little more than an idiot because in some of his entanglements he strikes awfully close to home.

I have been asked many times where I got the character of the Nutty Professor. He was born on a train from Los Angeles to New York. Planes were grounded due to bad weather and I had a show to do in Manhattan.

I was having a drink in the parlor car with some members of my staff when this little guy walked by with glasses perched on his nose. It was the first time I'd ever seen bifocals. He cleared his throat: "And ah, ah-hem."

I had a briefcase with stickers on it. He looked at it. "Are you show folk?"

I said, "Yes, we are. We're going to New York to do a show."

"Oh, marvelous. My name is Hartman. Surrealist Lunchbox and Stormwindow Company, Pittsburgh. I, ah, ah-hem. You make this run often for shows and skits and stuff?"

"Yes, we travel back and forth."

"Ah, say, that's marvelous. You going to have breakfast in the, ah, morning? Or per . . . ah . . . bef, ah, ah, ah, ah . . . you just going to see? Ah, get off?"

I bought him drinks for two hours; never took my eyes off him.

Many people can identify with him because somewhere, sometime, they have met the likes of him. He may even be a member of the family.

Having to handle both the serious and the inane, I think a comedy director is more flexible than a director who handles only drama. He may not be as profound or as solid as the dramatic director but he must know both areas. In knowing them, he will achieve a dramatic film as well as a comedic film. So far as I know, there are nine comedy directors in America. There are three or four comedy stars, as opposed to five thousand dramatic actors. It is a tougher racket for the director and the comedians.

I am not at all sure that good comic actors make good comic directors. If they are born comedy performers they have a certain flexibility which helps. A performer like Eve Arden, not born to comedy but a great technician at it, might well be able to step out as a performer and step in as a director. With all her experience and ability, she would not know until she sat in the chair.

There are fine comedy directors who were never performers. They brought in a feel for humor and a sense of comedy pacing. Norman Taurog and Frank Tashlin were never comedians. George Marshall and Frank Caper switched from drama to comedy but never performed. Many fine dramatic directors know how to handle touches of comedy. Hitchcock's sense of humor is incomparable. He uses comedy for relief of gripping suspense. No one does it better.

Mike Nichols went from comedy to drama, of course. His training and experience as a comedian will show through film after film. The slick *Graduate* displayed Nichol's comedy timing and pace, as well as the comedian's inherent feel for pathos. *Catch-22* called on other things from his bag of stage and television training as a performer.

How does one go about creating comedy for the screen? Better ask, How does one measure the ocean with a cup?

In *Modern Times*, Chaplin wanted to make a comment and he had a notion of how to make it. The "how" was automation, labor, management, the humanities—just dying to get the food on the table. His notion had a beginning, a middle and an end. Then he had to fill it up with gags within the context of what he wanted to say. Each gag said something.

I create my films in somewhat the same way: a notion, a beginning, middle and end; a spread of gags between. Let's take a simple one, a big briefcase. I put the briefcase on the table. I take out my shoes and socks, then a pair of boots, then a cat, finally a small pony; and button it up by taking out a smaller briefcase. People laugh. It's all incongruous.

I think and deal in visual terms, as Chaplin did, though I am not placing myself in his company. The benefits of thinking comedy in visual terms, as opposed to verbal terms, opens the door to incongruity and then to laughter. It is not just the visual joke, but who is doing it, why, and where they are doing it.

One of the most ingenious comic pieces in *Modern Times* took place in the department store. Chaplin was skating blindfolded. Graceful as a ballet dancer, he skated toward a danger sign. The moment he took the blindfold off and was made aware of the danger, he couldn't even walk. He became crippled from fear. I am certain that he wrote that huge skating sequence but not the *button*, not the failure of his legs. People were laughing at his take, "Oh, Christ, look where I almost went!" But the button, the inner block, the legs melting, was not written per se. It was an added visual thought, one of Chaplin's nuances.

To me, *Modern Times* is a very serious film. He illuminated the problems of a changing world. He made it look like a documentary but broke up the seriousness, camouflaged it, with sight gags. Chaplin was a comic film-maker, but as serious, in his intents, as any film-maker that ever lived.

Messages in comedy must be camouflaged very carefully. If the pace of the comedy is stopped for the message, then the film can be lost as well as the message. In the right frame of reference, on either side of the wildest gag, or within it, the social comment can be made.

There is no *must* for social comment in drama or comedy, and certainly a hundred minutes of laughter and pleasure is a message in itself. But if the audience can take something away with them beyond laughter, subliminally buried in their minds, then the comedy has served as great a purpose, sometimes greater, than the heavy-drama comment.

If the comic can berate and finally blow the bully out of the water, he has hitched himself to an identifiable human purpose.

16

THE VISUALS OF COMEDY

I've written some visual-comedy things with Bill Richmond that I believe are pretty insane. I'd like to think that twenty or twenty-five of them will go down among the better representations of screen comedy in this age. I suppose that twenty-odd exceptional visual jokes are not a lot out of the work of more than twenty-five years. Yet that might be about the creative average in any comedian's body of work.

I have my favorites, of course. One was in *The Ladies Man.* The Idiot is dusting and cleaning nearby a case of butterflies. He spots them. They're beautiful. He takes another look and opens the case. The five gorgeous pressed butterflies wing away, leaving five impressions in the case. The Idiot watches them go in a state of bewilderment. Finally, he whistles, and they all fly back to their impressions in the case. He shuts the door and walks away.

Another is when The Kid wants to take a picture of the moon at black midnight. He gets a flashlight, goes outside, snaps it on, and the whole city turns to light. Two people run out from under some bushes. "What time is it?" they ask.

These were written and carefully planned sequences but occasionally the joke, or sequence, is created on the set. In *Ladies Man,* I had a portrait of Helen Traubel over the fireplace and was again doing a cleaning-and-dusting routine. As I was setting up the shot, moving the camera to a low angle so I could pan The Idiot in, a light crossed Helen's portrait. It looked like a grease smudge was on it. I yelled to the prop man, "Clean it." But then I had a thought. "No, get me some lipstick." I painted her mouth with it.

In going for the take, The Idiot is dusting the portrait and when his rag touches it the lips smear all over the place. It was wild.

There is refinement of jokes on the sound stage and infrequently the lucky flash, such as the Traubel portrait, but most of it is written in detail and prepared well in advance of filming. Once I write a joke I give it to a sketch artist for rendering. I explain how I plan to shoot it, name the characters involved and estimate the camera moves through to the cut or dissolve. It is almost frame-by-frame planning.

I use the term "joke" to mean something funny, either verbal or visual, but there is a great difference between a joke, as such, and a visual-comedy sequence. I distinguish a joke or gag as being rather short and quick-cut. A visual-comedy sequence can be quite long.

Chaplin's conveyor belt sequence in *Modern Times* is clearly in the long category. At lunchtime, after working in the factory during the morning, his body is still animating from the movements of the conveyor belt. He goes outside and sees a lady with two buttons on her breasts. They have the same look as the bolts on the conveyor belt. His hands go for her. Obviously this is too elaborate to be called a gag.

There is a strict structure in visual-comedy writing. The comedy pieces are laid into the straight, non-comedic writing. If there are thirty visual gags in a film, they are paced out within the progression of straight storytelling. There is always a tendency to get the "cutes" and break the straight construction of a visual-comedy script, perhaps attempt to make it a solid hundred minutes of crazy. It never works.

Recently I collaborated with one of the best script constructionists in the business. He is not a comedy writer in the exact sense. He is a straight writer, but deals in comedy and creates straight situations. The comedy plays off them. This is where the comedy director enters with invention.

For example, in such a session we might have The Kid playing the role of a bank teller. We examine the possibilities. For openers, he gets locked in the vault. After that, someone passes him counterfeit money. He is nuts about a chick who comes in every Monday at exactly two o'clock to make a deposit. So there's a chance for the love interest. The necessary menacing factor might be the bank guard. He's been there forty years. He hates any kid, let alone The Kid. Before the session is over between the straight writer and the comedy creator, there are eleven things to do with the bank teller without ever leaving the bank.

In terms of invention on the set, comedy is little different from drama. Some of the finest moments of drama were not precisely in the script, though the groundwork was there. The same applies to comedy. Relatively, though, the comedy director has a wider field for invention. In comparing the two forms, he does considerably more set invention. A contradiction to that, of course, would be *The Odd Couple*. But the stage play had locked that story in, and the director was limited to additional cuts and punctuations.

Dramatic directors like Norman Jewison often add and invent tremendously with any piece of work. I read *The Cincinnati Kid* script and the pages were pretty good— Jewison took the material and made a great picture from it.

On the other hand, I have created gags or a situation that looked perfect on paper yet stopped the story line dead when cut into the film. On paper they read like they belonged in the structure. They also worked on the sound stage or I wouldn't have wasted the film. But in the editing room they got in the way. I have reels of this type of material, some quite good, that wouldn't work in many instances, because of the material around it.

Comedy, as such, has a completely different tone, though not necessarily a different form, in comparison with drama. It requires a different technique of painting, from the moment the script is in progress until the cutting stage. In drama the camera can be placed almost anywhere. In comedy the comic has to stay in the number-one position and the camera is locked to him. For instance, it is tough to go from a master shot to something cute and hingy when the character is being sold. All of the rules and constructions of drama apply to comedy, but there is an additional set of rules for the comedic form.

Quite obviously, different types of comedy are written in different ways. The Cary Grant slick punctuation of humor is not really visual, although his special character is visual. His humor comes from the script and is seldom invented on the sound stage. With his personality and skill, he rises above his material constantly, but the visual part of it, the mannerisms and facial delivery, is within Grant himself. Very few of the Cary Grant comedies will be remembered for dialogue or broad visuals. They will be remembered totally for his overpowering presence.

A classic example of the broad visual joke is Clifton

Webb's cramming of a bowl of cereal on the baby's head in *Sitting Pretty*. This an audience will remember, though possibly not recalling Webb—"Who was that actor that . . . ?"

There must also be relief from laughter as opposed to comic relief. An audience cannot be allowed to laugh too long, or too hard, within any one period of time. Rolling in the aisles comes from laughter but it also comes from the inability to handle it. People can become uncontrollably hysterical and the show is lost. Laugh too long, or too hard, and you can break a pipe. There are times when slight laughter is better than a lot of it.

If the laughter is extended too long, and becomes a discomfort, and the director must try to get the comic off the screen; drop back to exposition or plot. Then the comic can be reintroduced, and the audience returned to that moment just before aisle rolling. It takes as much care and timing to get him off the screen as it does to make him funny.

The Marx brothers used their musical numbers as relief situations. I also suspect they sometimes used them when they ran out of material. Mainly, it was for relief. Their material was fast-paced, particularly when Harpo was on. They moved so quickly that time had to be given for digestion:

Harpo is standing against a ten-story building. The cop asks, "You holding that up?" Harpo nods, "Uh-hmh." The cop says, "Screw!" Harpo walks away and the building collapses.

After that kind of piece, you just don't go to a thing with a banana peel. The audience must have some relief.

In another strange twist of our human existence, comedy comes out of violence, which is a brother to tragedy. The collapse of Harpo's building is violent; the guy walking into the excavation pit is violence. To the average audience, violence on the screen is a belly ripped with a seven-inch knife or a burst of machine-gun fire. They don't seem to notice the violence in comedy or stop to analyze the tremendous amount of it.

Probably the most violent comedic form is the kiddie cartoon. See them on a Saturday morning! *Road Runner* is worse than *Bonnie and Clyde*. If the kiddies want to get even with the boy next door, have them see *Road Runner*. "Ah-doo! Yeh, I'll get him."

When it's funny, the audiences reject the violence. Hire a circus clown to kill someone and then have the cops grill him. They'll laugh their heads off while taking the grisly information down. *Blondie* was violent; even *Fibber McGee and Molly*, on the radio, was violent. W.C. Fields was a master at violence. In a bank scene he almost choked a kid to death. "If your neck was clean, I'd wring it."

At times, Chaplin had a cruel, terrifying approach to comedy. He always kicked the fat lady in the ass after he gave the dog the last piece of sandwich. He never booted her before taking care of the puppy. In the first version of

The Cure, made in 1917, there was footage that would have destroyed him as a performer. In one sequence he passed a man with gout, looked around, swung his cane like a golf club and slammed that gouted foot. Then Chaplin smiled at the victim, pushed his hat over one eye and strolled on with that inimitable walk.

In the same film he helped a man who was having brake trouble with his wheelchair. Chaplin turned the chair so it would go down over a hill. The whole two reels were violent. *That* version of *The Cure* was never released.

Bonnie and Clyde was larded with humor coming out of the unfortunate, unintelligent minds of the two lead characters. They were very right for each other, and director Arthur Penn handled them with such skill and taste that the audience felt sad when they were killed. Twisted humor, sprinkled throughout the picture, helped that reaction. Clyde killed people because he thought it would be nice. It was sunny out.

In that kind of treatment I think the humor comes to the audience because of a certain fear of the characters. After it is all over, after fear has settled, a hollow laugh is the normal reaction to being backed into a corner by a guy with a shiv. There was laughter both hollow and genuine from *Bonnie and Clyde.* Penn, a former floor manager of mine, handled it magnificently.

Editing the dramatic film calls for good pace and timing but in comedy it becomes critical. Suspense films make demands on precision timing, but no category of film is as harsh as comedy. It begins on the sound stage to a greater degree than straight drama.

Most comics have the natural instinct to move one step beyond the joke—wrap it, button it, *then put the bow on.* When filming comedy, the bow must be there for no other reason than the dissolves.

Laurel and Hardy did not shoot the end of a scene simply because of the dissolve. They would let it go on. Stan Laurel kept it animating to prevent any chance of stagnant material during the dissolve—a five- or ten-foot hunk of film with the actor standing like a statue. They were seldom in trouble in the cutting room.

Again, it is a cardinal sin to cut the camera too quickly or have an actor go dead after he has finished his line and await the director's signal. I've yelled at them, "Say ear lobe, diarrhea . . . anything. Just don't stand there."

Performers like Don Rickles, the champion schizo of all time, will instinctively keep delivering until that last camera cut is heard. A very funny man, Rickles also has the comic's inherent greed to milk the last laugh, have the last line. They can be cut. There is no choice if they aren't on the film. He'll give a director more than he'll need.

It is all timing. In *The Nutty Professor* I had The Idiot talking to a strong man who was holding barbells in a Vic Tanney health-gym setup. The Idiot asks, "Are they heavy?"

I was shooting in a perspective to indicate The Idiot and

the strong man were of equal size, although the strong man was much larger. To punctuate the fact that something was going to happen, I began moving the camera closer to the confrontation.

The strong man answers, "Uh-hmh."

"Could I try?"

He hands the barbells to The Idiot. I stopped the camera to hold both of them within the frame. The Idiot has the barbells and they drop out of frame. I cut the camera and then made a shot of the arms, six-foot arms, extending all the way to the floor. Had I moved the camera, there would have been distraction. I had to stop early enough to prepare the audience for *thwump,* the long arms. Then cut to them.

It was an infinite cut, like a butt cut, delivering the joke instantly. The moment we rolled it on the moviola the barbell was there on the floor. It was there, *thwish,* with the long arms attached. It got a scream in the theaters. It all depended on the instant, infinite cut.

Usually it is not the cuts that are used but the cuts that are thrown away that make the jokes. There are times when a warehouse full of cuts won't do it. If it is not a workable joke, neither the sound stage nor the moviola will save it. The joke must be timed and mentally pre-cut on the set.

In *The Bellboy,* Stanley (The Kid) goes to the dog races with the other bellboys from the hotel. They get to the box, ready for the first race, and look around. No Stanley!

"Where's Stanley?"

"I don't know."

"Did you see him?"

"No."

A voice over the public-address system announces, "The first race has been canceled today. Sorry. Scratch the first race."

I cut outside of the dog track and there is Stanley walking eight greyhounds on leashes. The premise, of course, is that Stanley always walks the dogs for the hotel guests. I could have gone down to the cages and shown him taking them out one at a time. But that would have been a case of "show and tell" destroying the joke.

Comedy should not be edited for the periods of audience laughter. It should be cut exactly the same as drama. Cut to the frame line and on the visual level, rather than on a hunch that they'll laugh beyond the joke. (The comedy film-maker hopes the audience will laugh through and kill his next joke. He should be so lucky!)

It should be cut for pace, and there is no way to plan audience reaction—"Well, they'll laugh for so many frames." The footage of the joke can be stretched so the laugh is free to extend itself, but even that has its dangers.

If the audience screamed at a preview, and the film-maker is going to loosen his material so that the laughter doesn't cover the incoming material, he must consider that the theaters playing on a summer Sunday afternoon may have only thirty people in them. Thirty people don't laugh the same as four thousand. So he must cut it for pace and his own feel of the humor.

Neither can he cut for every audience in the world. For many years a large bulk of the business receipts have been foreign. The problem with the foreign audience and comedy is subtitling. The translation is always different from the original work. Very often, the humor, particularly if it is verbal, doesn't come across.

Occasionally there is near hysteria in America about the creative magnificence of a film. It goes to Europe, or Asia, and audiences there shrug, "It's good, but not that good." The interpretation is different; the translations are different. Fine European pictures have died in America for the same reason.

There is an expression in Yiddish that will make most Jewish people laugh. It is *Hak mir nit kain tsheinik*. Basically it means, "Don't annoy me." But the literal translation is "Don't hit me a tea kettle." If you repeat it to a Jew in English, he frowns back, "What is that?"

Whether it is subtitling or dubbing, fitting foreign dialogue to the actors' lips, translation is still involved. In dubbing, the trick, of course, is to fit the lines to the original actor's lip movement. It means either snugging or elongating. Something will be missing. The Italian word for face is *faccia*. The double syllable kills it right away. Pretty face is *bella faccia*, three syllables for four. There is no solution until the whole world speaks one language.

For European and Asian audiences, the only safe and

effective way of making comedies is by wide use of visuals. Yet the film-maker, unless he is doing pantomime, cannot gear himself to non-English-speaking audiences. If he is an American film-maker he must direct himself to that audience and hope his humor will be understood overseas. It will be, for the main part, if it is a good part visual.

17

THE COMEDIANS

I do not know that I have a carefully thought-out theory on exactly what makes people laugh, but the premise of all comedy is a man in trouble, the little guy against the big guy. Snowballs are thrown at the man in the black top hat. They aren't thrown at the battered old fedora. The top-hat owner is always the bank president who holds the mortgage on the house, or he's a representation of the undertaker.

In the early days, working night clubs, I learned that taking a pratfall in a gray suit might get a few laughs. But I had to get up quickly and start another routine. Take the same fall dressed in a $400 tuxedo and I could stay on the floor for a minute. They would howl when the rich guy took the tumble.

Or it is the tramp, the underdog, causing the rich guy, or big guy, to fall on his ass. In this respect the sources of comedy are a simple matter of *who's doing what to whom*. They include, of course, what the comedian does to himself.

Chaplin was both the *shlemiel* and the *shlimazel*. He was the guy who spilled the drinks—the shlemiel—and the guy who had the drinks spilled on him—the shlimazel. In his shadings of comedy, and they were like a rainbow, he also played a combination of shlemiel-shlimazel. In *Modern Times*, diving into six inches of water when he opens the back door, which is one of the great sight jokes in comedy-film history, he does it to himself.

My Idiot character plays both the shlemiel and the shlimazel, and at times the inter-mix. I'm always conscious of the three factors—done to, doing to self, and doing to someone else by accident or design—while playing him, but they are not in acute focus. They swim in and out at any given moment.

In studying Chaplin's films—where he is an aggressive character, protective character, defensive character, but always the center point—an erratic pattern emerges. I think this is because of his many shadings. In *Modern Times* he plays both the tramp and the underdog. While both are aggressive, they are not the same characters.

The character who opened the door and dove head first

into the mud was not the same character who was pushed by the cop. "None of that," he said. The latter character wouldn't have been so stupid as to dive into six inches of water. Often this type of shading is not written into the character. It is added, instinctively, by the comic.

In shadings and coloring, I think there are more demands made on the comic than on the straight dramatic actor. Although comics seldom perform straight dramatic roles, usually as a matter of choice, they have a relatively easier time in shifting to them than does the dramatic actor who is suddenly confronted with comedy. Many of the best dramatic actors lack a genuine sense of comedy know-how.

In the old days at the Palace in New York, when Eddie Cantor walked on the stage his sweet Jewish aunt would say, "Look at my Eddie. He *acts* like a dummy." And Eddie *was* acting. Milton Berle has done some marvelous acting roles. Jack Lemmon is a superb dramatic actor— *The Days of Wine and Roses*—as well as a damn good comedian.

The making of comedy is a very serious business within the dramatic structure of entertainment. On the level of pure performance, comparing comedy and drama, I think comedy is more demanding. The straight dramatic actor has his skills and emotional tools as does the comedian. But if he wakes up on a smoggy morning, stomach lousy and head full of aches, it is not too difficult to choke to death a while later playing Hamlet. The comic finds it somewhat tougher to turn on laughter if the world is funky and smoggy.

Stan Laurel was probably a near genius as a comic and as an authority on what makes people laugh. He was also a total film-maker. Toward the end of his career, after great self-schooling, he had become one of the finest technicians in Hollywood, in comedy or drama. I learned much from him, particularly in the last three or four years of his life. He was a moviola fanatic, a camera fanatic.

The directors who worked with Laurel and Hardy were confined to their ground rules, especially Stan Laurel's. Stan was the brains. Olie was a tremendous exponent, possibly equaled only by Harold Lloyd. He could do anything with Stan when the material was given to him. They were an almost perfect comedy combination.

Stan told me that Olie started looking into the camera, communicating directly with the audience, because he was never too sure what the next cue would be. He would take his cues from the script supervisor, who was always immediately to left or right of camera. Olie would roll around, get his cue, and then continue. It was effective, and they kept it. Although normally a legitimate "no, no" in film-making, it became one of their trademarks.

Even though they had writers, and Hal Roach Studios was overrun with them in the thirties, Stan did much of the writing. There was some bit of comedic genius in each film they did, and Stan contributed many of them. His touches, such as the hat that would elevate when he leaned against the wall and blew his thumb, are evident throughout their work.

He did a classic sequence in *Saps at Sea* where Olie would turn maniac if he heard horns. Placing the four or five pieces of trombone slides, timing the run around the boat with Olie to bring him to danger at the precise moment, was a near-perfect work of comedy pace and film cutting.

Stan understood the camera and what they, as a team, were doing visually in relationship to it. Much of their material played so well in the masters that they never dreamed of trying to match it in closer shots. The matching came from straight dialogue scenes where they could make a criss-cross or an over-on.

With visual slapstick content they worked loosely, because matching would have been impossible on many occasions. They moved from master head-to-toe, loose head-to-toe, to nothing more than a calf shot in some sequences. They wouldn't take the chance of restricting themselves because of spontaneity.

No material of consequence was out of the frame in their films. There was a lot of head room and air, left and right, in most of their compositions. It gave them space for spontaneous comedy, although their material was always written and prepared.

They finished their careers almost penniless. They weren't good businessmen and had no corporate setup.

Few actors bothered about business in those pre-tax days. And Hal Roach had them tightly corralled, anyway. Laurel and Hardy made a lot of money but kept little of it. Stan was married seven times and was always a soft touch. Olie was a barfly and a golf hustler. He left his dollars by the mahogany rail and on the greens.

Hardy died in 1954, and Stan was so affected by it that he had a stroke that same morning. After that day, Stan was paralyzed and seldom went out again. He couldn't bear the thought of anyone seeing him disabled. He told me, "Better they have the memory of fun." He stayed in his Santa Monica apartment from 1955 until his death in 1965.

Critical acceptance came late for Laurel and Hardy. It is one of the crueler stories of this put-on we're living in. The critics and the jet set seldom recognize something in motion. They wait until it is static or buried before they slowly creep out into the night to discover that once upon a time the masses enjoyed it. When recognition comes, the masses are busy enjoying a new, active thing.

I'll admit I can't wait to hear what is said about me after I croak. Being a part of the put-on, I'll also admit I'd like to go somewhere now to hear it.

Jack Benny is the best in the world at what he does, yet he is not a film comedian. His comedy is not for the visual medium in theaters for the world market. He can do TV specials that are very funny to an English-speaking audience, but they don't dig Benny in Rome. They do not understand buying one gallon of Texaco gas.

And any foreigner would have trouble really appreciating Bob Hope at his best. Hope has little competition at stand-up comedy. He makes no bones about the fact that his material is written for him, but no one else can put it across like Hope. The beauty of his talent is that he knows his limitations. His cream is monologue and he stays in that confine. He can't do a monologue on TV for sixty minutes, so he hits them for twelve and then goes into a sketch. Hope does films but depends on his character more than visuals.

Lenny Bruce was the most infuriating man I ever met in my life because he preferred to make his way with four-letter words. He was brilliant but couldn't make it as a straight comic. So he steered that brilliant mind into a joint with fifty-eight people. He could have swung with the best if he'd gone straight. I am not the enemy of Lenny Bruce, rest his soul, or the enemy of Mort Sahl. I am angry for them, not against them. I am angry with Andy Warhol for the same reason—wasting talent on so few, rather than working for the masses.

Harold Lloyd never touched my soul because nothing appeared to affect him, and I've never been able to include him in the category of great comedians. He was a great technical comic.

The great ones, the giants, are Chaplin, Stan Laurel and Jackie Gleason, in that order.

KIND OF A WRAP

I am moving more behind the camera. I have been taking pratfalls for thirty-seven years and my ass is sore. Going around to the other side gives a kind of satisfaction that I have never known in front of the camera, even with all the good things that have happened. I've been looking forward to the time when I can pass information to bright young talents and do it from the director's chair.

Hollywood is currently turning out less than a hundred feature films a year, and throughout the world not more than a thousand features are being made. Supply is short and demand is great. In the next five years, television will absorb forty-five hundred films. TV is where the new, young film-makers will get their breaks.

The major studios are now making films for television on a limited basis. Soon they will fully merge. There will be few or no theaters, and television will be the marketplace.° This newly aligned industry will have to turn to cinema classes and students for its pool of talent.

At present there are over five thousand directors and assistant directors in the Screen Director's Guild. But I believe it is just a matter of time—when the two industries are wed and bedded down, with home cassettes revolutionizing the exhibition phase—before there will not be enough film-makers available to meet the demands in Hollywood, much less New York or any other part of the country. The industry is on the threshold of great excitement and growth.

The new film-maker cannot take part unless he enters the industry with solid information layered over his creative drives. Imagination and natural talents will not suffice. Luck plays a minor role.

Antonioni wrote an article for *Cahier du Cinéma* on *Blow-up,* maintaining he lucked out on thirty minutes of the film. Formerly a still photographer, Antonioni did not go through an apprenticeship in making films. But he used his wide knowledge as a still photographer to compose his scenes in *Blow-up.* Antonioni candidly regretted he lacked the information to make it a better film. But it was not luck that created *Blow-up.*

° The Jerry Lewis Cinemas will produce approximately 3500 new theaters in the next five years.

Stanley Kubrick had the information to turn stupid lab mistakes into assets for his *2001: A Space Odyssey*. His last reel had an epidemic of mistakes in color gradations. He could have accepted the word of Technicolor consultants but his own information told him the experts were wrong.

He sat in the labs to make the last three or four minutes of that film. He was not guessing or asking. He told them, "Take the matrix and print it three ways and not together. Separately. And then keep it in negative form and I want to project it as negative. I want the blue and I want the yellow and I want the red, and I want the extensions of those colors in negative form broken down and projected in raw form. Don't put it together." It took Kubrick five years to make *Space Odyssey* and he traveled those years on his information. It was a brilliant film.

Breaks will come to the young film-maker, but unless he possesses at least rudimentary knowledge they will be of little use to him. Recently I saw a film made by a twenty-one-year-old, Steven Spielberg. It was twenty-four minutes of film called *Amblin*, produced for around $17,000. It rocked me back. He displayed an amazing knowledge of film-making as well as creative talent. He was signed to a director's contract by Universal. Even at twenty-one, he was ready when the break came.

The young film-maker must have confidence in his ability, but also know that he will face fear. There is never a time when I walk in front of a camera that I don't have 99 percent of my crew looking at me with some kind of envy: "Look at this confidence. Cocksure. What he knows he's going to do, he's going to do." They should only know that 60 percent is confidence. Forty is crap. But the 60 percent is so solid that it makes the crap look like 99.

Nervousness is important. Flop sweat is awfully good, but overwhelming fear in front of a challenge buries capacity and ability. It has to be licked with information.

My first solo directorial assignment was *The Bellboy*. I was scared to death. At the end of the first day I called my wife from Miami. I said, "I'm shivering. My nerves are out of my head. My nerve ends are six feet seven but I got through the day."

"How was it?" she asked.

I answered, "It was the biggest thrill of my life because I found out that all the things I wasn't sure I knew I knew."

What about the critics? Young film-makers should remember Goldwyn's line, "Don't pay any attention to the critics. *Don't even ignore them.*"

The world is still made up of green apples and dreams and wishing wells and throwing pennies in fountains; the heart beats fast when a pretty girl winks. All of that is still what it is all about. The important things, the ones some people put down, are the lovely, wonderful things that gives gooseflesh.

The young film-maker, with a desire to gain information and be the best in his craft, should also be thinking about puppies and apples and gooseflesh, and wonderful, happy endings.

About the Author

JERRY LEWIS has acted or directed or written or produced—and sometimes all of them at once—in more than forty films.

Twice he has been voted the Best Foreign Director of the Year by the French film critics.

His innovations, such as the remarkable set pictured on the back of this book, have been landmarks in the film industry.

He was born in Newark, New Jersey, in 1926 and has been involved in the entertainment industry for more than a quarter of a century—on the stage, in nightclubs, on television and in motion pictures. Mr. Lewis, his wife, and their six sons now live in Bel Air outside of Los Angeles.